Advance Praise for *Being Called to Change*

"The Teacher appears when the student is ready. If you are a student of the awakening of the inner self / soul, then this is the book to read! I have read many self-help books in my lifetime. Most have only one gemstone of wisdom to share—Dale's book is a goldmine of advice and tips to help anyone on the road to mastery. I look forward to sharing this book with my clients."

~ Dr. David Yoder, D.C., David Yoder Wellness Center

"Dale takes the complex concept of "Change" and shares with us why we avoid it, how it is inevitable, and the power that comes from embracing it. Dale proves his statement, 'change is inevitable, resistance is optional.' *Being Called to Change* is an entrepreneur's must-read."

~ Ken Courtright, Founder, CEO of Today's Growth Consultant, an Inc. 500 Company

"Dale nails it. His book reads like a spiritual life skills manual; he helps pinpoint what to pay attention to, what questions to ask yourself, and how to make the most imperative personal change at the right moment. You will learn to trust yourself and the flux and flow of life itself."

~ Crescent Orpelli, MA, MFT

"This book is a gift. It concerns daily life challenges and successes common to many people, so it will resonate with and motivate all who read it. Dale shares with us, through his life's experiences and the accumulation of his teachings, some of the most fundamental insights that can affect human potential. Initially, the reader will get actively involved with the transformational information and then will process it through the exercises found at the end of each chapter. This book is educational, interactive, and fun—readers will learn and prosper from it at all levels. What an inspiration and motivation for all."

~ Dr. Ronald L. Greenawalt, D.C., F.A.C.O.

"Knowledge of the soul and the ego is something we all need more of. Filled with wisdom and written in a way that's easy to understand, *Being Called to Change* is a book to be used as a powerful guide for becoming our best self. This is a life-changing book. It's about learning how to let go of those relationships and things in our lives that are no longer working, so that we can truly move forward. This book is amazing, and what Dale has to say on these pages actually works. I know this to be true, as he's been my teacher and mentor for years. He is the real deal."

~ Kym Figueroa, CEO of
Advanced Hair Health and Transformational Life Coach

"I've always taught, 'change or die, innovate and thrive'...so when I read Dale's new book, *Being Called to Change*, I was blown away. He offers a clear rationale, deep insight, and solid strategies for personal and professional transformation. Bravo!"

~ David M. Corbin, Mentor to Mentors,
Author, Keynote Speaker

"*Being Called to Change*, is an exceptional book, offering guidance for the spiritual seeker. It is lucid and offers deep and penetrating insights. I have known Dale for 20+ years and he is rare because he genuinely 'walks his talk' and his teachings and writing continue to be an inspiration to thousands around the globe. Dale is an excellent communicator and this is evident in his book. I am especially moved by how he cares deeply and listens to others with great respect, and by offering this book, he further demonstrates his caring and commitment to being a role model in the spiritual community. One of the things I admire most about Dale and his writing is how he continually examines his use of language and behaviors to consciously improve his own communication skills and foster relationships. Thank you, Dale, for offering such profound wisdom when it is deeply needed."

~ Ellen M. Laura, Author, Spiritual Counselor

"Are you looking for a day-to-day road map to transform your life? Then you cannot miss *Being Called to Change*. We live in a changing world and if we miss the boat we're left behind. I highly recommend that you read this book—and more importantly, that you put into practice the twelve Transformational Practices you'll find here. I love every part of this book and particularly "Become Who You Want to Be" because that is what you are really meant to be. We usually are so much more than we think we are! Dale is so inspirational...you won't stop reading until you are done!"

~ Dr. Danielle Chavalarias, CEO/President of InnerOptimal Inc.

"This is a transformational book. When we understand what change really is and how to actually embrace change, it truly empowers us. What Dale Halaway has to say in his book, *Being Called to Change*, really works. It's definitely a must-read."

~ Spectacular Smith, Founder & CEO of Adwizar

"Through his teachings and this book, Dale Halaway is bringing answers, order, and simplicity to a complicated and confusing world. When I first met Dale, I realized it was time to wake up to this repetitive cycle of just existing that was no longer working for me or my family. In my ten years of being immersed in his teachings, Dale has become my personal mentor and friend. In a world full of charlatans and inauthentic teachers, I can say with great confidence, through years of personal experience with Dale, he really is authentic.

Being Called to Change is not filled with theoretical concepts. It's filled with a lifetime of discoveries and practical tools that Dale not only developed, but uses daily. I've never met anyone so dedicated to their own personal evolution than Dale Halaway. His work has become a game changer in my life. He has helped me to wake up from an existence of sleepwalking. It has not always been an easy or comfortable process to wake up, but oh how wonderful it is to stand wide awake and walk in the sunlight! This book has the power to begin a movement of consciousness like I have never seen in my lifetime. Thank you, Dale."

~ Matt Lewis, CEO/Executive Producer of SimonWill Entertainment

BEING CALLED TO CHANGE

DALE HALAWAY

The information in this book is not intended or implied to be a substitute for professional medical advice, diagnosis or treatment.

DEDICATION

Mary

To my beautiful mother...while you are in my heart, I still miss you.
I so wish you were here to enjoy this.

Randi

To my precious daughter...You have helped me to stay on the path
and your own transformation has been such an inspiration to me. I
am very proud of the woman you have become, and what you have
accomplished. So, it's with much gratitude and respect that I lovingly
share this with You.

One and Only You

Every single blade of grass
And every flake of snow,
Is just a wee bit different...
There's no two alike, you know.

From something small like grains of sand
To each gigantic star,
All were made with THIS in mind...
To be just what they are.

How foolish, then to imitate
How useless to pretend,
Since each of us comes from a mind...
Whose ideas never end.

There'll only be just ONE of ME
To show what I can do,
And you should likewise feel very proud...
There's only ONE of YOU!...

~ James T. Moore

CONTENTS

FOREWORD

by Dr. Enid V. Singer, Ph.D., LMFT

Dale Halaway is an emerging thought leader, passionate entrepreneur, devoted father, inspirational trainer, stand-out life and business coach, and an alchemist for transformation. He has logged more miles than anyone I know on the journey of soul-evolving inner work. In years bygone spiritual seekers and adepts renounced worldly pursuits and material acquisitions and chose celibacy. They frequently chose retreat to far-away places for hours of meditation and contemplation in efforts to quiet the mind, remove distractions, and access the Divine. Dale is a modern-day adept. He has really achieved the extraordinary in not removing himself to the mountain but finding the mountain within while parenting, doing business, nurturing relationships, and living successfully in the world.

Dale has discovered and articulated easy-to-understand ways of categorizing Core Life Issues and what we do in life that sabotages forward movement. His examples are clear and his tone compassionate which makes us willing to identify our own self-defeating patterns. We all have them. His book could be used as a manual for helping one answer not only the perennial question, "Who Am I?" but "Who Am I Becoming, and Who Do I Want to Become and How?" He makes some of the best distinctions between ego and soul-self I've come across. I've read many a psychology textbook and Dale's deep dive especially into the "Needy Self" and its consequences will be useful not only to those ready for transformation but those facilitating it—therapists, life coaches, teachers, trainers, and the like! There has been much focus on needs in both classical psychology works and self-help books and on feeling worthy of meeting one's needs. Dale takes us down a richer path, he explores deeply to uncover what fuels the need, what dynamic pushes the need to the fore. He makes a significant contribution in suggesting we practice self-inquiry and lift the veil on the core issues that drive the need. At the close of each chapter Dale provides stepping stones inward with incisive questions we can ask ourselves. The book is as much a "practicum" as it is a book.

I wish Dale would have spoken more about himself and his journey in this his first of what is sure to be several books. Because he didn't, I want you, the reader, to know a little about the author. I think of Dale as a "tracker" for the Soul. What I mean by that is that the author has made it his mission and part of his life's work to seek and follow the trail of signs pointing the way to Source, the Divine, which on his own journey, necessitated peeling away all that was irrelevant. While on the path, he consciously had stripped or stripped himself of everything most of us use to keep ourselves feeling safe including country of origin, health, relationships, home, career, identity in the world, and money in the bank. I've witnessed him let go of things one never imagines being able to live without. Both his life and body have been his laboratory. His is a bold journey and his readers now are beneficiaries.

He does what he asks his readers to do—be with what is; don't turn away, don't distract, don't run, don't avoid; when necessary, surrender. Anyone who knows him well will say he "walks the talk" and is an embodiment of authenticity. He has been willing to enter states of consciousness that most don't or won't, affording him invaluable knowledge and wisdom. What he brings back for all of us lucky enough to know him as friend, mentor, teacher, trainer, or now author encourages us to redefine life and success on our own terms. He inspires us to bravely confront and overcome our demons and play a bigger game in life.

Dale has the knack for designing learning experiences and posing questions that help us illuminate our shadow, those things we have tucked away in the back, in the dark, under the rug of our psyche. He has decades of creating sacred, safe space in meetings, trainings, conferences, on the telephone or in person. He now does that with his book—he creates for us a safe place to take a deep dive within with likely rich reward. He is a master at creating a culture for growth and transformation.

Get ready for a breakthrough—or plural. I had a big one while reading the book. This year I have been remodeling my home and before reading Dale's book, it was known as "the remodel from____" (you can fill in the blank). I have had months of snafus, mistakes, outright incompetence, and almost everything had to be done twice and one thing five times. Needless to say, it was hard to be upbeat. In the middle of the book an awareness broke through! It felt as if I had suddenly awakened to the realization of untold blessings, meetings, events, and knowledge I would never have known had it not been for the remodel journey in exactly the way it has unfolded. This wasn't a Pollyanna realization; it is a deep truth. I couldn't tell you which concept or question spurred my ability to see the very same phenomenon from a diametrically different lens but something in the reading made it so. There was a transformation of something painfully frustrating and disappointing to something about which I am patiently more grateful. There are books that "work" on you while you read them. This is one of them.

Be forewarned, this is not the kind of read most do in one sitting. In fact, don't be surprised if you find yourself taking breaks. Inner work is not for the faint of heart. I found myself doing the very things Dale talks about but then returning anew. Sometimes it's not comfortable. Take time, take a walk, write, come back, dive in, self-reflect. Dale has curated many practices that will assist you in awakening, up leveling, breaking through, transforming, healing and ultimately successfully answering the Call to Change!

Dr. Enid V. Singer, Ph.D., LMFT
Certified Trauma Specialist

The Transformation Trilogy™

The Transformation Trilogy™ consists of three books with a common theme—transforming yourself into the person you were always meant to be.

The first theme in the trilogy is *transformational change*. What is change? How do we embrace it (instead of resisting it) when it comes knocking on our door? How can we let go of that which is no longer working in our lives? If something isn't working, why isn't it easier for us to let go?

The second theme is *achieving our greater destiny*. What is destiny? And, more importantly, can we affect our destiny? If so, are we affecting it in a positive way or a negative way? Where and how does choice or free will come into play? And, does karma have anything to do with our destiny?

The third theme is *manifesting dreams and realizing goals that are in alignment with the soul-self*. Can we consciously create our own reality? If so, why would we manifest something that's negative and painful in our lives, rather than creating something wonderful and positive?

By applying the innovative principles and unique processes the author shares in this trilogy, you can become the person you were born to be!

TRANSFORMATION
Trilogy

Begin Your Transformation:
www.DaleHalaway.com

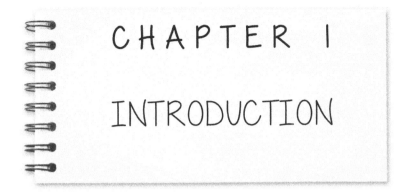

CHAPTER 1

INTRODUCTION

This book is about change. It's about discovering your true self. In these pages, we look at how to embrace change by challenging your ego-self head-on and empowering your soul-self. The soul-self is your "true self," the ego-self is your "false self," and the key to making real change in your life is to learn how to conquer the ego-self and re-connect—and stay connected—with your soul-self.

The soul-self thrives on change, it welcomes change, because the soul knows that self-evolution is vital for wellbeing. The ego-self spins illusions, it manipulates us into believing that change is dangerous, that we are fine just as we are. But if we want to attain our hopes and dreams in life, we must confront the ego, move through its barriers, and engage with our true essence—our soul-self. The soul-self knows who we are and where we are going; it does not resist change, it celebrates change. The soul-self knows that by changing from the inside out, by becoming our best selves, we not only transform ourselves, we change the world.

Life is a series of constant, undeniable, and unavoidable changes. The universal constant throughout the world is change. It's the thing we all know for sure—as the Law of Change states—one way or the other, everyone and everything will change. It's natural to change or transform. The caterpillar transforms into a butterfly, the acorn transforms into an oak tree, the baby's body into an adult's body. Nature teaches us that if we're not growing, we're dying. We're either becoming more positive, powerful, and productive or more negative, weak, and destructive. Some people have become so fixed and rigid within their own consciousness and live their lives in such negativity that they bring more strife, struggle, and stress upon themselves. To truly grow, we must change our ways—from the inside out.

The foundation of all progress is transformational change. No matter how masterful we become at whatever it is we do, or how successful we become, there will always be something to change. Everyone can totally transform something about themselves—we all have the inner power to do so. When we tap into our soul-selves, we learn to welcome change and to let go of the ego's resistance to change. We get confident, energized, we move forward in our lives and manifest the lives we are meant to live.

The wisdom in these pages will show you how to trust that your higher self knows what your ideal life is—and how to attain it. You will learn how to reconnect with the part of yourself that knows how to live beyond the ego, in the realm of spirit. Your soul is calling to you right now, encouraging you to embrace your true purpose, to rise to your fullest potential, and to transform your life.

We can learn a new and more proactive approach to inviting and embracing the dynamics of change in our lives, personally and professionally. Are you ready to answer the call to change?

Are you ready to answer the call to change?

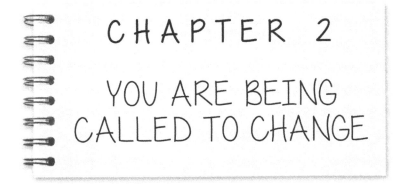

CHAPTER 2

YOU ARE BEING CALLED TO CHANGE

S ometimes we're so stressed out, we're ready to have a heart attack—or at least a panic attack. When we feel stressed, it's because we're not aware of the root cause of the stress. So, it grows, and over time, it comes to define our whole way of living.

Once we get into this pattern, it's natural to turn to something to numb the pain and calm the stress we're causing ourselves. Our drug of choice could be candy or ice cream, alcohol or drugs, sex or gambling, even compulsive shopping. Whatever it is, it's a coping mechanism. But the problem is, numbing behaviors don't address the cause of stress. They treat its symptoms. Soon enough, we forget there is any other way to be. Habits and coping mechanisms are, by and large, non-productive and they can quickly become destructive. Once stress becomes a lifestyle, it's lodged within our very cells.

Now, stress can be beneficial. In fact, if we confront the source of our stress within the structure of a transformational method (see later), stress can be incredibly productive. This is what's known as *eustress,* or the type of stress that can be harnessed for constructive purposes.

This book is an invitation to those who are living with stress and who may be terrified to think of living life differently. It's about discovering the patterns and feelings that promote stress, tunneling down into them, and discovering what messages they have for you. It's about letting go of resistance and embracing all those things in your life that keep you trapped and stagnant. It's about changing from the inside out. It's about listening to your body, vanquishing your ego, tapping into your soul, and along the way, transforming everything you are in order to become who you want to be. The call to change is really the call to return back to your natural state in being your truest, most authentic self…your soul.

Maybe you are stuck, snagged where you are. You may not have made changes in your life in months, even years. In this book, we'll delve into the phenomenon we call "subconscious resistance" and learn to identify the causes of your stress and how you may be contributing to resisting change. Maybe you've tried other forms of personal development or have attended transformational seminars. Maybe you feel as though only another seminar can help you progress on your journey, but here's a little secret: personal development seminars can function just like a hit of your drug of choice. They may seem helpful, but they're just keeping you numb to the root of your distress. In short, this book is an outstretched hand: *Are you ready to transform?*

Every person comes into the world with a purpose.

Every single person comes into the world with a purpose, a person they are meant to become. Most people start out intending to become the person they were meant to be, but they get derailed. And when I say *most*, I'm talking about ninety-nine percent of people on the earth. We get off course, we become unconscious to our higher self, and that unconsciousness leads to other life problems, those lead to further unconsciousness, and we find ourselves in a tangled maze of troubles. Whether we are unconscious, off course, or just unaware, it can take a long time to unwind ourselves from the maze—I know it took me a long time.

The most important question we can ask ourselves when we begin our transformational journey is, "Am I becoming the person I was meant to be?" This marks a checkpoint; it's a question we must ask ourselves throughout the course of our lives. This question raises other questions. "Who am I becoming, really? Am I motivated by love and inspiration? Or am I driven by fear and desperation?" These are simple questions but when you start to ask them daily, you begin to realize you're on the path to becoming someone you don't want to be. In this book, we will explore what to do with that realization, and how to empower yourself to make changes and get back on the right path.

When you ask yourself, "Am I becoming the person I was meant to be?" every day, you're putting yourself through an ongoing self-examination process that's gentle yet consistent. It's a process that never stops until you become enlightened—that's the reality.

The World of the Uncomfortable

Change is inevitable, resistance is optional. Change is going to happen, whether we like it or not. The deeper question is, in what way will change *change you*? Will it change you for the worse? Will you allow change to make you sicker, more negative, poorer? Will you become weaker in the process of changing, or stronger? Will you work in tandem with the Law of Concentration to harness change and use it to make yourself more positive and healthier?

We can always resist change, and most people do. When we resist the changes that life brings us, it's because we're afraid to relinquish control. Changes come into our lives to improve it, but when we react to change fearfully, if we believe that change means losing control, we resist. You may think that by resisting a situation, you're taking control of it, but in reality, you're just making it worse. In fact, living in a state of fear and resistance creates a whole host of problems, and before you know it, you're living in a maze of destructive behaviors that you created. Resisting change is how we find ourselves ten years down the road saying, "I feel hopeless. I feel like I'm in quicksand. I feel like I'm dying. I feel like I can't get out." It doesn't happen overnight, it happens over time. Ultimately, your life reflects the energy you put into it, so if, through your thoughts, words, and actions, you plant the seeds of negativity, resistance, and fear, your life will become overgrown with those things. You'll feel powerless, hopeless. "What's the use? I'm never going to get out of this. I might as well settle for fourth best; my best days are over."

Resistance is ultimately a pushing-away energy or a pushing-down energy. When we're resisting someone or something we're pushing them or it away. If we don't want to experience a feeling, we push it down, we resist—consciously or unconsciously. Perhaps we resist because we're afraid of dealing with our feelings in a responsible way. Or, perhaps we're afraid that if we were to stand up to someone or something, the resulting conflict might spin out of control and someone might reject us or make us wrong. What might that look like? Imagine, for example, somebody starting their own business. It's not going well. No matter how hard they try, they end up back where they started. It feels like doors are always closing on them, like someone is intentionally making things difficult for them. This person feels as though they're being acted upon from the outside, but the reality is, *change comes from within.*

In this book, we dive into the concept of unconscious resistance and discover that the truth is, nobody else is pushing us: we're resisting change. As we wander deeper and deeper into the maze of our lives, we become less and less aware of our true selves. We have to: if we were to maintain our higher consciousness, it would hurt too much. It's already painful to exist in this state: that's why people turn to their drug of choice. We can go on like this for some time: wandering further and further from the path we're meant to be on, numbing ourselves to the pain we're experiencing, always wandering further afield because we deny the truth: we are holding ourselves back.

At some point, though, something happens. Something rouses us from our stupor. It's happened to you—something nudged you to pick up this book. All of a sudden we realize, "Oh my gosh! What am I doing? All this time I've been resisting change in my life and now I see I've been making it worse!" After this awakening, we begin to recognize, bit by bit, that we have another choice—we can deconstruct the maze. It is just a matter of recognizing the two core parts of the human experience: the ego and the soul.

What are You Empowering?

We'll discuss the nature of the ego and the nature of the soul later in the book, but for now, suffice it to say that the ego-self is our lower self, the part of us that leads us astray. When we awaken to the fact that we're in a maze of our own creation, it means we've been empowering the ego-self and neglecting the soul-self. The soul is your higher self, the greater version of you, the true version of you. But if you're completely under the influence of the ego, you will have lost any connection to your higher self, to your soul. You've gone unconscious, so of course you just continue, moving forward blindly, until you're lost, not knowing which way to turn. This is the pivot point for change! You can be still, find your center, and then retrace your steps. You can walk straight through your self-created web of chaos and onto the path of change, that place from which you can right yourself and get back on track to becoming who you were meant to be.

The truth is, getting back on the right path is a long journey. Your quest is to connect with your soul. You have to develop a relationship with your soul; get to know it. This is a major project—most of us spend more of our lives in our ego than in our soul. But just because you've been empowering your ego doesn't mean you know it. To come into alignment with your soul, you must first learn what makes your ego tick.

It's a big deal to acknowledge that we've been empowering the ego instead of the soul. How can we distinguish whether and when we are serving our egos to the detriment of our souls? What, specifically, empowers the ego? What empowers the soul? And, what is the difference between the soul and the ego anyway? Well, as noted earlier, the soul is our "true self" and the ego is our "false self."

Put simply, the ego is not real. It's a fabrication we build up from a set of beliefs we pick up over time. We learn these things from our parents, their parents learn it from their parents, and they from theirs. So, you see, it's no use blaming your parents for your unhealthy ego—we all learn from our environments. You could call it emotional inertia: it's the result of allowing the same destructive patterns to carry on through generations, unaddressed.

The reality is, we live in a world powered by ego, in which the soul long ago was relegated to the shadows. But we have the privilege of liberating it, bringing it back into the light, doing the transformational work—and maybe even succeeding at setting ourselves and our souls free. If we do this illuminating work, we will be the luckiest beings on Planet Earth. We will be free to embody our true self, our soul-self, which is a powerful thing.

Losing the Ego, Embodying the Soul

Consider, for a moment, the belief that we have power over another person. We see that belief playing out all around us—in business, in politics, in religion, in families. This is a false belief. But if you believe that you can have power over another being, that's how you will live your life. Of course, once we have released the soul from the ego's dominance, we recognize that the soul would never behave in this way. So, we realize that beliefs and behaviors that advocate oppression are ego-based, and are indicative of a loss of connection to the soul-self.

Another ego belief is that the world is inherently dangerous. When people believe that the world isn't safe, they act out of fear. If we believe that everything is a threat, we protect ourselves and push away the things or people we perceive as dangerous. But some people have turned their world into a safe space, so why can't everyone?

When we grow up believing the world is a dangerous place, we may not believe it could be different. Then, someone comes along and shows us something different, and we see new possibilities. Suddenly others are doing impossible things, and so are we, and soon what was inconceivable is practically commonplace. Suddenly, we are strengthening our soul, finding our way past the controlling ego, taking charge, creating our world anew. Here's the deal: strengthening the ego is an unconscious process, but strengthening the soul takes work, consciousness, and dedication.

Should we choose to strengthen the soul, it will be because there is someone in our world—a family member, a dear friend, a teacher, a mentor—who has already made that choice. Once you have a role model, you can choose to bring your life into alignment with your soul. It's important to remember that we were born as a soul into a body. The ego, however, has to be created at some point during our early life. Then comes the choice as to which one—the soul or the ego—we will choose to support. What we choose can have a lot to do with the environment we grow up in. Obviously, if everybody in our environment has already lost their way, it will be easier for us to wind up nurturing our egos and resisting the call to become our true selves.

We were born as a soul into a body.

In my work as a transformational teacher, I've found that there are three types of people: those who have lost their connection to their soul-self, those who are on their transformational journey, and those who are in alignment with their soul-self and have fully embodied their soul—or at least have crossed a threshold on their journey and there's no turning back.

They are well on their way to embodying their soul-self in this lifetime.

If we're in the first group, we might feel like we're living inauthentically. In fact, we may feel like a fraud, or like we're shallow. We've lost our connection to our soul-self but once we start reconnecting, we slowly but surely bring our life into alignment with our higher self. We may still have moments of inauthenticity; we may backslide into damaging behaviors. But still, little by little, we're able to connect with feelings of beauty and grace, the way our life was meant to be. During this transformational time, we are able to recognize when circumstances activate the ego—and we can do something about it.

Then there's those who have been doing transformational work for some time and have made this work a lifestyle. Because it's so ingrained in their daily lives, they experience the soul in a whole new way. The soul slowly but surely takes over their bodies, their minds, their personalities. They live their lives more simply, and they feel truly at ease with themselves.

Learning About the Ego

When we lose our soul connection, when we distance ourselves from the person we were meant to be, the ego comes into being. Along the way, we get so disconnected from the soul that we forget we have one, or we believe incorrectly that our ego *is* our soul. In other words, we can no longer tell the difference. Egos are like human beings—they learn, and some become very smart over time—so the ego can imitate the voice, the feel, even the look of the soul. It can make you believe you are acting out of your higher self, but no matter how you cut it, it's not your true self. It's your false self.

Which brings us to one of the traits of the ego: the ego maintains supremacy by sustaining our disconnection from the soul, its objective is to distract us. When somebody is really under the influence of their ego, they'll often take on some mission or purpose that they believe to be their life's work, but then two or ten or fifty years later, they come to the painful realization that it wasn't their life's work after all. Other times, the ego will distract us with a relationship. We'll meet someone and believe we've found a new business partner or a new lover or a new friend, when in fact, that relationship is just a distraction the ego is dangling before us to prevent us from realizing our true selves. The ego wants us distracted, because until we're able to see the ego clearly, we can't control it. Until you can recognize the machinations of the ego, you cannot transcend it. So, the ego will continue to parade distractions before us in an ongoing attempt to lead us further from our true path.

The ego will get us to react to situations in a way that only creates further distraction. If I go into a highly reactive state, for example, if I scream and yell and judge and criticize, I will push away the people I love, maybe the people I value most in the whole world. In other words, the ego compels me to sabotage my relationships in order to produce unnecessary problems that will induce further poor decision-making.

The Master Key to Real Change

Change is an ongoing process, a lifelong progression towards enlightenment. As you learn about the principles of personal transformation and integrate them into your life, you will be empowered to make better choices—and that is how you will grow to your fullest potential and become the person you were meant to be.

The Laws of the Universe

I was completely enthralled with studying and teaching Universal Laws back in my twenties. During the course of what turned out to be an almost ten-year run, I discovered more than fifty laws. These laws are unchangeable, impersonal. Universal Laws don't care if we use them. We can't change them, just as we can't change the law of gravity or the law of electricity. What we can do, however, is learn about them and, more specifically, choose to work with them. Should we choose to resist them, violate them, or misuse them, there will be consequences—just as there will be blessings when we choose to embrace them, respect them, and work with them responsibly. It doesn't matter whether we are aware of them or not, just as it doesn't matter if we're not aware of the law of electricity. Place your finger in an electric socket and you'll get zapped. It's that simple. The Laws of the Universe work 100 percent of the time, all the time, every time. I will reference eight laws in this book:

1. **The Law of Change** says that everything and everyone will change. It's in the natural order of life to change, for better or worse. The only constant is change.

2. **The Law of Evolution** states that it is our soul's natural state to evolve. To not evolve is to deny the soul its actualization and expression.

3. **The Law of Transformation** says that we are responsible for our own transformation. To mature, to grow, and to evolve, we must learn how to let go of all that no longer serves us, as a way to transform ourselves (personally and collectively).

4. **The Law of Correspondence** states that As Within, So Without. The outer landscape of our lives is a direct reflection of our inner landscape. This law also says, As Above, So Below. The world below matches the world above.

5. **The Law of Accumulation** says that a small thing, done repetitively over time, can become a big thing. Whatever that small thing is, good or bad, if it is done over and over again, it grows in strength.

6. **The Law of Concentration** states that whatever we concentrate on (positive or negative) will grow and expand into our day-to-day lives.

7. **The Law of Opposition** says two things. That which we oppose, we strengthen, and whatever is opposing us can also strengthen us.

8. **The Law of Increase** states: That which we praise, increases. If we honor and celebrate our victories and accomplishments, we can expect the good in our lives to expand. Similarly, if we give attention to the negative, that too will increase.

 **Exercises**

For the exercises below, take some quiet time by yourself. Get still. Picture your higher self.

If you don't have an image of your higher self or your soul just yet, picture the words "Higher Self" on the screen of your mind. Place these words right over your heart. With your journal and pen in hand, read these questions. Go with the first answer that comes to you—write it down. Over time, the answers to these questions will change as you change. Be authentic. Stay in the moment—and breathe!

1) How do you normally deal with stress in your life?

2) Have you used a "drug of choice" to deal with stress or negative emotions? If so, what has your go-to drug been? How often do you use it?

3) Based on how you've been living your life, who are you becoming? Are you becoming the person you were meant to be? On a scale of 1 to 10 (1 being very little, 10 being a lot), how much of your life has been motivated by love and inspiration? How much of your life has been driven by fear or desperation?

4) When you think of your "ego," what do you think of? What do you see? Has your ego ever sabotaged something you've valued? If yes, what was sabotaged and how did the sabotage happen?

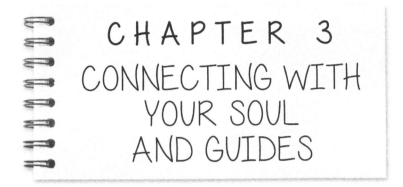

CHAPTER 3
CONNECTING WITH YOUR SOUL AND GUIDES

Becoming Aware of Your Ego

It is the nature of the ego to disapprove and to not accept things as they are. There is always someone or something it cannot accept. This is how the ego keeps you stuck: as long as you are unable to embrace the conditions of your life, you cannot move forward and grow.

Connecting with Your Soul

You weren't born a body, you weren't born a mind: you were born a soul. On the physical level, you are the product of your biological parents, but your soul has its own history. Your soul has characteristics unique to you, and in this chapter, we will learn about the different aspects that make up each person's soul.

A soul has both masculine and feminine qualities. To discover the essence of our soul, we must first reacquaint ourselves with masculine and feminine characteristics. The masculine, for example, is intellectual, it's the thinker, it carries the active principle. The feminine, on the other hand, is intuitive, it's the feeler, it carries the receptive principle. To find joy, we must balance our masculine and feminine energies and learn which characteristics are most applicable to any given situation. If we are parenting a child, for example, it might be in everyone's best and highest interest to bring out the feminine side of the soul. Similarly, if we are building a skyscraper, it might be a good time for our masculine characteristics to take the lead. Ideally, we will nurture both sets of behaviors so we can be successful as parents, spouses, partners, friends, or professionals.

Some souls are new,
some are old,
some are ancient.

Our souls have an age. Some souls are new, some are old, some are even ancient. Older souls have experienced many lifetimes in this third-dimensional world, and the transformational seeker can learn, through self-assessment and through various metaphysical processes, to access that soul history and give context to their current lifetime. Gestalt therapy, rebirthing, bioenergetic breathwork, mindfulness meditation, shamanic dream work, and other such holistic therapies can help seekers to delve into their unconscious minds to retrieve soul memories.

There are different types of souls, just as there are different ethnic groups here on Earth. In the soul realm, there are Indigo, Golden, and Crystal souls—spiritually and technologically advanced souls who are being born into all the nations on our planet to champion spiritual and scientific advancements around the world. And, just as we're from different nations, we're from different star systems. We all have a soul family of origin: maybe we're Pleiadean, Arcturian, or Sirian, to name just a few. What we have in common, though, is that we are all a part of

G*o*d—or whatever name you choose to call the Creator. This is where our true spiritual power comes from. As we reestablish the connection with our true soul-self, we begin the process of returning to our soul, and then, we eventually become the walking embodiment of our soul. It's from this place that we discover the real power of our soul, which is what truly empowers us to design and create our life in a way that becomes profoundly meaningful, joyous, and fulfilling.

The same holds true with connecting to our guides. So often, we forget that we are surrounded by spiritual helpers who are here with us to guide our journeys, to help us come into alignment with our soul-selves. We all have these guides and as we begin to get reacquainted with our souls, we also come into contact with these nonphysical helpers.

Children are often quite connected to their guides. In fact, they often see them, speak to them, and draw great strength from them. Parents often shut this down, telling their kids they're just making things up, imagining things. But of course, the children know their heavenly helpers really are there! Indeed, our guides are always with us, nudging us in the right direction, giving us the opportunity to change course should we choose to. If we should find ourselves straying from our path, if our ego drives us to behave badly, develop addictions, or push away our loved ones, our guides will create the conditions for us to become conscious again.

Connect with your guides and your soul, and your life will become brighter. Life will take on a different meaning for you. You'll find yourself letting go of things you never could have imagined living without. Maybe you thought you would never go without your glass or two of wine every night, but now it doesn't seem so important, you find yourself craving a nice vegetable juice instead. Maybe you have a pattern of cheating on loved ones, but as you bring your ego into alignment with your soul, you find yourself cherishing your beloved in ways you never had before. It's amazing, and it happens naturally. It's the natural progression that occurs when you are really connecting with your soul.

Just like the ego, the soul has its own characteristics. The soul is a spark of the divine creator that dwells within us, our 'Godspark.' In fact, our soul is the part of G*o*d within us, and it is the part of us that draws us towards self-actualization, higher desires, and genuine love. The soul knows the truth of everything, and when we learn to connect with it, we gain access to the soul's universal knowledge. The ego is self-centered, but the soul is the centered-self. The soul is forgiving, loving, and approving. It is our source of fulfillment. It lives in the present moment. The ego feels it is the victim of outside events, but the soul sees the purpose in everything. The soul responds to whatever life brings, it inspires others, just as it is inspired by others.

When we embody our souls, we give up the title of General Manager of the Universe: we no longer believe it is productive or even possible to control people or events. Rather, we are grateful for everything and everyone around us, because we know that we are the lucky ones. We are the free ones. Where we once thought about how we might like people better if they sorted themselves out, now we simply accept and love people for who they are, and where they are on their journey. The soul is receptive of higher teachings and greater truths. The soul thrives on change, it welcomes change, because the soul knows that evolution is necessary for growth. Our souls are attracted to simplicity, harmony, and peace.

The way of the soul is humility and compassion. Whereas the ego is self-important and critical of others, the humble soul knows that everyone has their own struggles and is deserving of compassion.

As the wonderful writer, Neale Donald Walsch, states in his seminar, *Living From Your Soul:*

> *The human soul is a direct expression and a singular individuation of Divinity, much like a drop from the ocean is both part of the ocean but not the entirety of the ocean itself.*
>
> *The soul entered into physicality, or the individual reality of each and every one of us, in order to create an unlimited experience of divinity, not a limited experience of humanity!*

To put it another way, the soul is here on a mission from G*o*d. That mission is to reveal the totality that is G*o*d, with a direct experience of what it means to be divine.

 ## Exercises

For the exercises below, take some quiet time by yourself. Get still. Picture your higher self.

If you don't have an image of your higher self or your soul just yet, picture the words "Higher Self" on the screen of your mind. Place these words right over your heart. With your journal and pen in hand, read these questions. Go with the first answer that comes to you—write it down. Over time, the answers to these questions will change as you change. Be authentic. Stay in the moment—and breathe!

1)   Is there someone or something you are having a challenge accepting? Who? What? And, what is it about that thing or person that has been a challenge?

2)   Do you feel that you are a "new soul" (i.e., as in a "first-time soul") or an "older soul" (i.e., do you feel you have been here many times)? In conversations with others, are you ever referred to as an "older" or "younger" soul?

3)   What are five characteristics of your soul?

4)   Have you ever acted like the "General Manager of the Universe" in your life? If so, in what way and with whom?

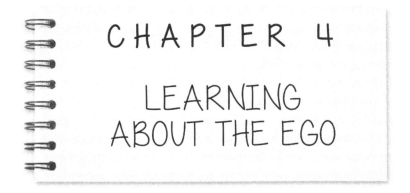

CHAPTER 4

LEARNING ABOUT THE EGO

Our soul is the larger version of us, whereas the ego is the smaller version. The ego is a fabrication, a set of false beliefs. The ego believes that we have power over others, and that the world isn't a safe place. The ego compels us to push away people and things we perceive as a threat.

Should we choose to strengthen the ego, we do so unconsciously. Should we choose to strengthen the soul, we do so consciously. That means that in order to strengthen the soul in our bodies, we've got to wake up. We've got to become more conscious of the negative dynamic that's running through our planet right now. It would be utterly impossible to be awake, to be conscious, and still decide to give strength to the ego-self.

Your Soul Connection

Most of us believe our life is about success, prosperity, happiness, health, and love. But we didn't enter into our bodies here on earth just to achieve those goals—and many of us haven't yet entertained the possibility that there might be a deeper, more profound truth as to why we are here and what it means to live through our soul-self. In some ways, waking up to our soul-self is like the famous line at the beginning of the *Star Trek* movies: "...To boldly go where no man has gone before." We are going to the frontier of the soul.

It all begins when we realize we have lost our connection to our soul. For example, there might be someone who believes their life is all about their romantic relationships. Love is wonderful, and we all ought to experience it. But if we approach love without a soul connection, we're pushing, trying, forcing things—and we destroy the very thing we most desire.

As mentioned earlier, there are three types of people that come to my seminars: those who have lost their connection to their true soul-self and don't know it; those who are in the process of reconnecting to their soul-self; and those who have truly begun the soul embodiment process.

Those in the first group are living their lives on automatic pilot. They repeat the same things over and over again. They take the same route to work every day, never considering what it might be like to change the scenery and purposefully take a new route. Those in the second group are waking up to their soul-self, becoming conscious to the truth. Slowly but surely, they're making decisions that bring them back into alignment with their soul-self. This group is making rapid progress, they embrace change as they recognize clearly that as they get better, their life gets better. They might run into an old friend, someone they haven't seen in a while, and that old friend might remark how healthy they seem, how positive their life has become. The change is visible in them. Those on this transformational path celebrate change.

Then there's the third group. In alignment with their souls, those in this group are in a deeper process of returning to their true selves, and their souls are slowly but surely inhabiting their bodies. Those in this group may lose old friends, because their friends aren't yet able to join them on their transformational journey.

The truth is, we all have a connection to our soul-selves. We are born connected to our souls, but because of our childhood or our environment, we do not learn to stay aligned, we stray off the path. Being misaligned creates space in us for the ego and its misconceptions to take control. We cling to false beliefs because it's painful to recognize that we've lost our way. As I often say in my classes, "We create a maze of complexity in our lives when we hold onto things we should really be letting go of."

What Does Your Ego Want?

In order to connect with your soul, you must first understand the ego. How does the ego operate? What are its tricks? What does the ego want?

To connect with your soul, you must understand the ego.

The ego is the lower, undeveloped part of us. The ego operates in the realm of lower desire, what I call *needy energy*. The ego plays tricks: I call this *the trickster* or *the magician*. The ego spins illusions. It's never satisfied. It's self-centered and judgmental. It makes us believe we're making progress when in fact we're wasting energy, standing still. The ego is afraid, it's disapproving, it thrives on misery. It lives in the past and the future and keeps us from connecting to our present moment.

The ego is the part of us that tempts us, it prods us into inappropriate reactions. We might lose our temper or have a tantrum, because the striving ego needs to create negative consequences. Living from the ego is living falsely.

Many people over the years have told me that when they start to connect with their ego, to understand it, they feel how superficial their life seems. It's an uncomfortable realization. Their ego tricked them into believing their life was real, but their transformational work has shown them how far they have strayed from their true selves. To understand why the ego impacts us in negative ways, we must grasp the truth—the ego is afraid. Fear has a place, of course—one only has to walk down a dark street alone to understand the value of fear—but that's fear based on a current moment. The ego is afraid of the past and the future; it makes us feel tense about things that have no bearing on the present, things that have long ended or are yet to come. Similar to fear, the ego thrives on control. Put the ego in a foreign situation, one it can't control, and watch it react in its most damaging ways, ways developed from a life lived in fear.

When the ego gets activated, fear takes over. It enters the physical cells of a person's body and that person feels the fear as though it were real and present. They might go from appearing strong and calm to acting frightened. When the ego is activated, it does everything it can to shut down the experience. Restricted breathing is usually the first thing that becomes noticeable—the rhythm of the breath shifts, the chest becomes tight. Some people literally hold their breath—for a couple of minutes at a time—and when they do breathe in, their breath is short and shallow.

Depending upon the influence the ego has over an individual, the outcome of such fear-based physical reactions will be different. Each ego has its own patterns, its own systems, but those systems don't function consistently every time they get triggered. Consider, for example, the salesperson who has a sales routine he's developed over time. While he may follow his routine with no modifications for some customers, he recognizes intuitively when a potential customer might not respond well to Step 3 of his routine, or Step 5, and he adjusts accordingly. The ego is the same way. As you study yourself through transformational work, you begin to recognize your ego's destructive patterns, whether or not they are precisely the same in each instance. As you become aware of the patterns, you develop the skills to interrupt them and can reroute that egoic energy towards other, better, thoughts or actions.

While each person's ego is unique, there are some universal tricks that, once recognized, can help break your ego's damaging cycles. I refer to these as *The Ways of the Ego*. They're all related, and ultimately, they

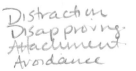

keep us in a state of fearful resistance. But it is worthwhile to explore each Way thoroughly, so you can recognize it when it activates in your own ego.

The Ways of the Ego to Keep you safe

The first way of the ego is *distraction*. The ego loves to distract you from what you truly ought to be doing in your life. Your distraction becomes your direction, and once you're distracted, you can't connect with your soul. And, if you do manage to complete a task, there will probably be consequences and you'll need to clean things up. The ego loves to keep you busy cleaning up messes you never would have made had you been on the right path.

The second way of the ego is *avoidance.* For example, it's easy to ignore one little bill or one little tax form, but once you ignore that first one, the task of handling the next one becomes monumental. Soon, avoidance has led to financial ruin. It's hard to connect with your soul when your bills aren't in order.

The third way of the ego is *manipulation.* This is where the ego's needy energy comes into play. The ego loves to use your needy energy to get you to lie, cheat, and convince people of what they otherwise wouldn't believe, all from its self-centered desire to have things go its way.

The ego also manifests through *exaggeration.* The ego will take something good in your life and blow it up, make it look larger, because it plays right into that needy energy to look good. The ego can also exaggerate the negative, causing you to spiral into shame, anger, or depression.

The ego is also *deceptive,* with others and with the self. As a trickster, the ego can get us to believe that we're a lot further along on our path and we can attempt to convince others or ourselves of this false progress. Yet, if we really are that far along, we will see results to back up our belief—and results never lie.

The ego is also *disapproving.* If, for example, we see ourselves as better than others, we'll notice things about them that we disapprove of. If we see ourselves as less than others, we'll notice things about ourselves that we disapprove of. And, if we are unconscious or unaware of our ego's disapproving tendencies, we'll consistently be on the lookout for something in others and/or in ourselves to make wrong or disapprove of.

The ego *projects* onto others responsibility for things that we cannot yet see in ourselves or be accountable for in our behavior. For example, perhaps we have abandonment issues and we believe that others are exhibiting abandonment behavior towards us when really, they remain supportive in ways we do not recognize. Or, perhaps we project our dreams onto another person and expect them to adopt our hopes and expectations, behaving as though what we want is what they want for themselves.

The ego seeks *immediate gratification*—everything is about being gratified *now*. For example, say someone who is ego-driven comes into money—they have to spend it right away. This person's ego always needs *something*—more attention, more action, more help, more time—more of everything, right now. They do not honor what's right here now, regardless of whether it's someone else's time or money or their own. This gratification-seeking ego drives addictive behaviors—it needs that next rush, that next exalted (false) feeling. Until this ego gets healed, it cannot be satisfied. No matter how much you give it, it will always want more.

The ego has a way of *discounting* important events in our lives. For example, perhaps we have a profound experience, receiving guidance from someone—advice that we know in our bones is right for us. Or perhaps someone does something powerful for us. Shortly thereafter, however, we discount the guidance or deny the potent experience. When our ego discounts things in this way, we can avoid going deeper—into discovery of the self, or into relationship with another person. If the ego can stop us from moving forward and transforming our lives, it will do so. Period.

The ego loves to *isolate.* We can separate ourselves from things and others in our lives not because it's healthy, or because it's the right thing to do, but rather because we're exhausted, trying to make our lives, our relationships, our businesses, and/or our careers work. Perhaps, for example, we've been trying to make something happen that hasn't been happening, or perhaps we've been hurt in a personal or business relationship and we are carrying unresolved pain or anger around what happened to us. But isolating ourselves from others does not solve these problems, it simply creates a new problem. Once we are isolated, it might even look like we've resolved the pain or anger. But then we find ourselves in the pain of loneliness. We disconnect from what's going on in our world and we separate from our true soul-self.

The ego also loves *attachment*. If we are not conscientiously aware of our ego, it will guide us to become attached to situations, business projects, or relationships that ultimately will never work. And, once we are attached, we can get stuck. The ego celebrates stuckness—it wants to be where there is no forward movement, for as we have seen, it is in *stasis* that the ego remains safe.

But you see, the ego is just afraid, it's not evil or bad. It just wants to protect itself. It perceives itself—and you—as being under threat, so it uses whatever tools are at its disposal, even when those tools are flawed coping mechanisms that don't address the root cause of the distress. We are not to hate the ego or seek to destroy it: what the ego really needs is love and understanding. The goal of transformational work is not to eliminate the ego, but rather to heal it so that it can be lifted up and integrated into the soul.

The goal is not to eliminate the ego, but to heal it.

As people learn about the ego, they identify its tricks, they figure out how their individual ego operates, what triggers it, and what patterns repeat when the ego is driving. Little by little, they break patterns, they consciously respond rather than unconsciously react to situations in a more soulful way, bringing the ego closer into alignment with the soul. When we harness the ego's frightened energy, we feel lighter, happier, beautiful, liberated. As we wake up and welcome the changes in our personal and professional lives, the soul slowly begins to assimilate the ego. The soul takes over as it integrates what the ego has learned. Once the soul starts to have its way with us, we begin to experience a rebirth of our true selves—we heal, we change—and our lives literally transform as the ego becomes one with the soul.

 **Exercises**

For the exercises below, take some quiet time by yourself. Get still. Picture your higher self.

If you don't have an image of your higher self or your soul just yet, picture the words "Higher Self" on the screen of your mind. Place these words right over your heart. With your journal and pen in hand, read these questions. Go with the first answer that comes to you—write it down. Over time, the answers to these questions will change as you change. Be authentic. Stay in the moment—and breathe!

1) Think of someone you feel has not been connected to their soul. What do you see? Write down what you see.

2) Which one of the three groups noted above resonates most with you? What is it about that group that resonates with you?

3) How would you describe your ego? What are three characteristics that clearly depict your ego?

4) What is one of "the ways of your ego" (e.g. immediate gratification, avoiding, isolating, etc.)? How does that "way" play out in your life?

5) What can trigger your ego? For example, does someone have to say something (perhaps in a particular way), or do something (like cut you off in traffic) to make your ego flare?

CHAPTER 5
THE SIGNIFICANCE OF PERSONAL TRANSFORMATION

Transformation is the key to real personal growth and spiritual evolution. Let's remember the Law of Evolution, which says that it is natural for our soul to evolve. By not changing and evolving, we prevent the soul from actualizing. There can be no forward movement in our lives without transformation. Transformation is the process of letting go of what is no longer working, to create space for something new.

In my classes, I always ask, "On a scale of one to ten, how comfortable are you with change?" Most people say three or four, a few say six or seven. I've never come across anyone who says ten. If it's a challenge for us to let go of things that are no longer working, our lives become heavy. If we hang onto things that are no longer good for us, our lives become so heavy we can feel like we're being pulled into a dark vortex. Doing more of what isn't working isn't going to make things better, advancement depends on getting comfortable with letting go.

For, example, say it's time to move to a new house or office. How many times have you moved? What was your experience like the last time you moved? Typically, how easy or natural is it for you to move? Once you know it's time to move, do you embrace it or avoid it? Do you come up with reasons why you don't need to move now or do you usually say,

"Let's do this?" Throughout the years, I've often heard others speak in dreadful ways about moving. Heck, I've had my own challenges with it as well—until moving no longer challenged me. That's because not only have I moved many times but at some point, years ago, I started to become conscious of what it was I was doing that was making the moves dreadful—I was resisting.

We resist moving because it's an uncomfortable process. It brings up things we don't want to look at or deal with. It challenges us. The truth is, if something doesn't challenge us, it doesn't change us. And moving presents an opportunity to let go of things that are no longer serving us. As we do, we create space for something new to enter our lives. Our new home or office always looks so refreshing. Once we're on the other side of the move, it can feel like a new start. Once we've unpacked and settled in, we suddenly discover, we've stopped resisting—we've let go.

If something doesn't challenge us, it doesn't change us.

Developing the ability to let go is the key to transformation. The Law of Transformation reminds us that to mature, to grow, and to evolve, we must learn how to let go of all that no longer serves us. When we let things go—a home, a relationship, a career, our finances, our health habits, our beliefs—we create the space to welcome the next stage in our lives. Now, practicing letting things go is like building a muscle: if we don't exercise it, it atrophies. Tapping into our ability to let go awakens us to the fact that we have the power to improve our own lives. As that "muscle" gets stronger, as we get more comfortable with releasing harmful habits or relationships, we become more empowered to make bigger, better changes down the road.

The first step to making change is accepting that you are responsible for improving your life. Many people come to my workshops believing that it's someone else's responsibility to heal them. But as you dive deeper into self-discovery, you come to the same conclusion that every seeker before you has come to: the longer you resist taking responsibility for changing and the longer you drag out the transformational process, the longer you force yourself to suffer. The truth is, only you are responsible for your own wellbeing. The only one who is going to change you—is you!

The famous Russian writer Leo Tolstoy once said, "Everyone thinks of changing the world, but no one thinks of changing himself." It's true: so many people work hard to change their family, their community, their city, the country, or even the world. In reality, if enough people paid attention to transforming their own lives, the world would change.

Recognizing the Call to Change

The Greek philosopher Heraclites once said that "the only thing that is constant is change." But while change is the only sure thing we can rely on in life, still, many of us struggle to recognize when we are being called to change. Even if we do understand on some level that change is needed, too often, we allow fear of the unknown to prevent us from acting.

We've all watched it happen: perhaps a friend is being pummeled by life, and we want to shake them and tell them they're missing something that would fix it right away, but we know they have to figure it out on their own. More often than not, if someone is resisting a change that may be obvious to an outsider, it's because that person doesn't feel safe enough to accept the new conditions of their life.

Sometimes life brings us big changes. Everything gets turned upside down but then, out of the blue, a new opportunity arises. Maybe it's a promotion, maybe we move our business to a new city, maybe a new romance is on the horizon. Change can also come in the form of an accident or a break-up, and while such changes can shock or upset us, in the end, all change provides the opportunity to do something new. All change brings growth. I've recognized that there are five key signs that it's time to make a change, which I present to you in order of their intensity.

The first sign, the subtlest, is a sense that something is about to happen. It could be any kind of change: personal, professional, financial, physical, emotional. It's like when animals sense an earthquake before it happens. Before the financial crash of 2007/2008, for example, some intuitive people sensed that a shift was about to take place. Of those who felt that tremor, some had the foresight to prepare, others dismissed the feeling and suffered the consequences. This first quiet sign presents itself primarily to those who are more in touch with their soul, those who have developed the capacity to pay attention. As always, even recognizing the precursor to change makes it easier to embrace change when it arrives.

The second sign is more intrusive. We notice that something isn't working the way it used to. If a career change is coming, we notice ourselves making more mistakes or becoming apathetic. It's easy to ignore these small indicators, to dismiss them as insignificant, but they are telling us that it's time to let go of something that's not right for us anymore. Again, an intuitive person might be able to recognize these signs, let go of what's not working, and make space for something new, but others will have to wait for the louder, more painful messages before they awaken to the call to change.

The third sign is that doors begin to close. When they do, it's obvious that things aren't working, but we only reach this point if we're so averse to change that we'll do just about anything to cling to the problem we are entrenched in. Here, relationships at work might fall apart. People we thought would never leave us vanish from our lives. We can't figure out why things aren't going our way; we try desperately to get this person to stay or that person to come back. We try to force our business to stay afloat as our clients fall away. We're meant to shift into a career that would attract a newer, better clientele, but we're so terrified of losing what we have, we can't see it.

The fourth sign is that a new opportunity shows up out of nowhere. Sometimes life or the universe will shake things up by disguising the opportunity with a crisis—and it's in the crisis that we discover the new opportunity. Or, sometimes, we're pointed in a new direction through a relationship or career prospect.

The fifth—and brightest—sign that change is upon us comes in the form of intense, vivid dreams. If change has been coming for us and we have resisted, we begin to have dreams where our loved ones disappear or our home collapses or something big is uprooted. Change is coming no matter what, and if it has to, it will invade our dream space and force us to listen.

Another way to understand the varying calls to change is through the metaphors of a feather, a brick wall, and a Mack truck. Some people—the intuitive ones—will recognize a subtle call to change, such as a feather floating to the ground in front of them. What an easy, pleasant way to discover that it's time to change! But if you are oblivious to what's happening in your life, it may take a more abrupt approach to get you to pay attention: say, walking face first into a brick wall. Clearly, this is an unpleasant way to be informed that something in your life needs to change. But if the impact of that brick wall isn't enough to get you to change course, at some point a Mack truck is going to be coming towards you at seventy-five miles an hour! At that point, there is just no going forward and even the least intuitive person on earth will be forced to change tack.

As we do the work of personal transformation, it becomes easier to hear a call to change. We may feel it before it arrives and be ready, the door wide open, to welcome it in. When we treat change as an honored guest, the change process is less frightening; we can appreciate it as the gift it is. But if we are less aware, we might need change to come knocking on our door before we can acknowledge it. We might be wary, but we've had experience; we can adapt when we open the door and find change standing before us. But if we are truly unconscious to the fact that we are being called to change, change will come pounding on our door or blasting our house open, and we will be terrified.

As it's happening, change can be painful, deeply upsetting, even scary. But as we develop the capacity to examine our lives from a higher perspective, we find real joy in welcoming change. After all, change is inevitable, it's part of our journey to self-actualization.

Symptoms of Unconscious Resistance

What if we could recognize a call to change before someone pounds on our door demanding that we adjust our life path? What if we could prepare for change so that when it comes, we know to open the door of our lives and welcome change like an old friend? If we could make space for change, we wouldn't have to be afraid anymore.

The key to preparing for change is to check for unconscious resistance. Of course, if we're resisting, we're likely not even aware of it, so we have to know it by its signs. Resisting change takes a lot of mental energy, we always have to be on guard, so we're constantly exhausted just living our lives. We feel drained. We're pushing people away, pushing our emotions down, pretending we don't notice the signals. Our souls are speaking to us: something in our lives isn't working and we need to make space for something new! But we're scared to let go, so we struggle to hold onto what we have, even when it's increasingly obvious that what we have is not in our best interests.

Earlier, we discussed the dynamics of the ego and the soul: when we ignore the signs telling us it's time to let go, the ego, that frightened base instinct, takes over and wreaks havoc. This creates more signals that we can spot only if we're searching for unconscious resistance within us.

You might be resisting change unconsciously if you're pushing hard, pushing someone away, or pushing something down inside yourself so you don't have to confront it. You might be resisting unconsciously if you find yourself reacting, screaming, judging, condescending, or spinning out of control. You might be resisting unconsciously if you're living in a perpetual state of want, always chasing the same thing and never getting it. People commonly demonstrate this resistance by making the same New Year's resolution every year, never acknowledging that whatever they're doing isn't addressing the root cause of their desire.

You might be resisting if you are being controlling, micromanaging others in order to force life to be the way you want it. Controlling as a form of unconscious resistance often crops up in the business world, where, for example, a boss might not be aware of how much pressure they're putting on their subordinates. Controlling energy is common in relationships too, it frequently forces the controlling person's partner to pull away, to seek respite, even if they aren't ready to end the relationship.

And if we're not sure whether or not we're resisting, we can always check in with our bodies, as they will tell us when we're in unconscious resistance. The body will manifest a tight or tense energy in one or more of these three areas: the throat, the center of the chest, or the solar plexus. We'll revisit this later on in the book.

The sooner you learn to identify areas of your life where you are exhibiting symptoms of unconscious resistance, the sooner you can stop resisting, let go, and embrace the positive changes life is bringing.

The Importance of Letting Go

The soul is responsive to the winds of change.

Once we begin to notice resistance, we must begin to accept and embrace change. Again, resistance is rooted in fear, and fear is the calling card of the ego. The soul does not resist, the soul flows; the soul is responsive to the winds of change. Once we uncover what it is that we're being called to change—whether it's our career or our love life or any number of other things—we find the courage to let go of the old, unproductive thing and celebrate the potential for something that can bring us joy. In other words, to make space for that new, beautiful thing, we must get comfortable with leaning into that wind and letting go.

Should you resist the winds of change, and cling instead to the painful shreds of familiar routines because you are scared of the unknown, you will find facing the prospect of change painful. The more you resist, the more painful and prolonged the process of change will be.

As discussed earlier, you—and only you—are responsible for letting go of what's not working and you cannot wait for favorable conditions. For example, imagine someone who has decided to untangle herself from a romantic relationship that is no longer bringing her joy. Ideally, the separation would be mutually agreed to, and if it is, the split will certainly proceed more quickly and less painfully. It's wonderful if both people are willing to participate in the process, but it's not necessary. But many times, only one person can see that a relationship isn't working anymore, but the other is still hanging on. The process of ending the relationship will take longer in this scenario, and it will be more painful, but it's still necessary for both people to move on to the next good thing that's waiting in the wings. By initiating change, you ease the process of transformation, and diminish the potential for pain, both for yourself and for your relationship partner. For whether they knew it or not, the only option was to let go. Change was inevitable and hanging on would have caused far more pain and heartache—over a longer period.

So, this brings us to a powerful question: Are you living in a state of letting go or a state of hanging on? One of these states is conscious and one is unconscious, but if you do some careful self-examination using the information in this book, you can notice the subtle signs that change is upon you.

If we are living in a state of letting go, we're surrendering; if we're in a state of hanging on, we're resisting. If we're letting go, we feel secure; if we're hanging on, we're insecure and anxious. If we're letting go, we're flowing and flexible; if we're hanging on, we're blocked and inflexible. If we're letting go, our thoughts move and change; if we're holding on, our thoughts are circular, going nowhere. If we're letting go, we're open to creativity and possibility; if we're hanging on, we're restricted. If we're letting go, we allow those around us to live in their own way; if we're holding on, we force others to conform to our ideas about them. If we're letting go, we trust in ourselves, our partners, the universe, our G*o*d; if we're holding on, we're suspicious and mistrustful of everyone. If we're letting go, everything about life gets simpler; if we're holding on, relationships and endeavors become unmanageably complex. If we're letting go, our self-confidence increases; if we're holding on, our self-doubt increases. If we're letting go, our body feels relaxed; if we're holding on, our body becomes tight.

Are you holding on or letting go?

 **Exercises**

For the exercises below, take some quiet time by yourself. Get still. Picture your higher self.

If you don't have an image of your higher self or your soul just yet, picture the words "Higher Self" on the screen of your mind. Place these words right over your heart. With your journal and pen in hand, read these questions. Go with the first answer that comes to you—write it down. Over time, the answers to these questions will change as you change. Be authentic. Stay in the moment—and breathe!

1) On a scale of 1 to 10, how comfortable are you with *Change?* Mark that number in your journal. Why did you give yourself this rating or number?

2) Have you been trying to make something work in your life that hasn't been working for you? What is it?

3) If you were being called to change something about yourself, or something about how you've been living your life, what might that be?

4) How easy has it been for you to recognize when change comes knocking on your door? Based on your experience, do you require the "feather only" approach, or do you wait for the "brick wall" or "Mack truck" experience?

5) What do you notice when you are resisting someone or something? What do you notice when someone else is resisting someone or something in their life?

CHAPTER 6
HOLD ON AND SURVIVE, LET GO AND THRIVE

Earlier, we listed the characteristics that define holding on and letting go. Suffice it to say that everything that is good (or, everything that is "G*o*d") belongs to letting go. Letting go means surrendering to what is, abandoning resistance, and allowing our soul's energy to carry us in the direction we're meant to be going. When we surrender in this way, our lives become blessedly simple. I've always said, "A life of complexity is produced by the ego, a life of simplicity is produced by the soul." You can be sure that if your life is a tangled web of complexity, you've allowed your ego to lead you astray.

In my seminars, often I encounter people whose lives are one big maze of complexity. They've gotten into the habit of finding short-term solutions to their problems instead of dealing with them for good, and they feel overwhelmed. They are surviving rather than thriving. They've lost the ability to let go of people, behaviors, and things that are no longer serving them. The fact is, change is inevitable, and letting go of the old to embrace the new is a constant challenge. Our generation struggles with it, our parents and grandparents struggled with it, our children will struggle with it too. Our ego wants us to cling to the familiar to avoid the uncomfortable, and it will never stop: letting go is ongoing work to be practiced with care, like a gardener lovingly pruning their roses each spring.

In a way, change is like the seasons. Without winter, there could be no summer, and, without the hard, cold season of letting go, there could be no time to plant seeds, or to harvest the fruits of our labors.

The first step to living in a state of letting go is learning to recognize when we're not—that is, our first objective is to examine where in our lives we might be clinging to old, broken arrangements that we know, somewhere deep down, aren't working. Awareness is the beginning of letting go. *↗ My family / Meg*

Holding On? Letting Go?

Whether it's a person, a thought pattern, or the quiet knowledge that it's time to make a change, the more we struggle with some aspect of our lives, the more power it has over us. So, this element of our lives becomes thornier, harder to manage—and as we know, complexity is the product of the ego and simplicity is the product of the soul. As a soul, we want to thrive; as an ego, we want to survive, just doing enough to get by and maintain the status quo. Struggling against truth empowers your base aspects; surrendering to change moves you closer to the ease and simplicity of your true path. Think of it this way: that which we oppose, we strengthen—which is the Law of Opposition.

Consider, for example, the loops of negative thinking so many of us suffer from. All it takes is one little poke at our self-confidence and we spiral into damaging self-talk. Maybe our whole day is ruined because we've allowed ourselves to slip into the well-worn track of self-blame, self-recrimination, and self-doubt. A thought gets stuck, and paradoxically, the more we try to dislodge it, the more entrenched it becomes. In other words, engaging with negative thought loops is a classic form of hanging onto them. The way to release ourselves is to surrender. Acknowledge that the thought is there, that it is painful, and then allow it to flow through you and away from you. The more you practice this simple shift, the easier it becomes, until suddenly you realize that a thought that once might have disabled you for days is now hardly noticeable. You've let it go.

The way to release ourselves is to surrender.

Another example: Perhaps it's time for you to clear an outstanding debt with a person or an institution. You've been thinking about this for a while. You've known it's time but you've been putting it off, and now the pressure is mounting. If you had come clean with this debt as soon as you knew it was time, you could have saved yourself unnecessary hardship, but now the whole thing has snowballed into all kinds of subsidiary problems. You're not ready to commit to the clearing yet, so you resist, hanging onto the familiar rather than surrendering to the unknown. (Now, what does that sound like? The soul, or the ego?)

One more example before we move on: By holding on, you are struggling to control the uncontrollable. Imagine, for example, a boss having difficulty with an employee. The boss, not having done his transformational work, feels the need to control the employee to ensure he does his work correctly. The employee, understandably feeling scrutinized, is more likely to make a mistake, not less likely. Cue the vicious cycle: the boss remains angry, the employee's work isn't perfect, the boss exerts even more control, with an increasingly damaging effect. But if that boss had done transformational work and recognized that his controlling behavior made matters worse, he would have encouraged his employee to learn and grow by assigning them a challenging project—and would even have celebrated the employee's failings as an opportunity for growth. In the second scenario, the boss has let go of trying to control things and has found himself in control. As soon as he steps out of the way, the process moves more smoothly. Consider too, the emotional ramifications of these two scenarios. In the first, a controlling boss feels insecure and doesn't trust either himself or his employee; in the second, boss and employee gain self-confidence and trust one another, which will be helpful going forward.

Relax, Surrender, Let Go

In my coaching work, I often say, "Life really begins once we let our soul have its own way with us." We know that holding on is ego work and letting go is soul work, so now we can take a beautiful short cut to connecting with our soul. What we have to do is let go of everything that no longer serves us.

So, how do we do that? How do we do the terrifying, uncomfortable work of letting go of the familiar and the unproductive? I use a mantra: "Relax, Surrender, and Let Go." I speak it over and over to myself during the day until it becomes the drumbeat underneath everything else: "Relax, Surrender, and Let Go." Over time, holding these three simple ideas in my mind changed both my understanding of and my relationship to the mantra. If you practice the ideas embodied in the mantra, your body will revert to its natural state of surrender. Mantras have a unique power to affect not only the physical body, but the emotional, spiritual, and mental bodies of the energy field as well, resonating outward with the call to let go.

I offer a more in-depth guide to letting go of what no longer serves us in my TransCovery Process® which is part of my transformational life coaching system. You can read more and watch a video about how to let go on my website, *www.DaleHalaway.com*

Original Pain, Unnecessary Pain

I've heard it said that, "There are two types of pain: one that hurts you and one that changes you." I've given the two types of pain different names: original pain and unnecessary pain.

Original pain comes in many varieties. Original pain is everything from stubbing a toe to graduating from high school: this is inevitable pain, part of being alive, and it may even mean that we are growing. Original pain comes to us because we are growing, and it's not a bad thing. It hurts, of course, but with a dollop of self-reflection, it becomes clear that this is pain we can learn from.

Unnecessary pain is far worse, and it exists only as a result of our refusal to feel original pain. Talk about unconscious resistance! Any time we try to numb ourselves to the pain in our lives, we create unnecessary pain for ourselves further down the road. Pain has to be addressed: whether you do it now, when it's simple and productive, or later, when you've allowed it to bourgeon into a ferocious beast, is up to you.

Let's explore some examples of unnecessary pain so we can identify it in our own lives.

Imagine you've had a friend for years, and that the friendship has brought you joy, solace, and growth. But recently, you've noticed that every time you see this friend you come away feeling depleted, bitter, angry, or perhaps doubting your self-worth. This is original pain: it's the pain of realizing it's time to move on. And yes, the leaving will hurt, but it will be so that you can grow and find greater joy in new relationships. But if you are not ready, if you cling to the increasingly toxic remains of the old friendship, you will create unnecessary pain for yourself (and probably for your friend as well).

You can think of original pain as growing pain. We all experienced it in our childhoods, the feeling of our bones stretching inside of us, the feeling of our adult teeth pushing out our first set. It hurts, to be sure, but it means we're growing up. We also experience metaphorical growing pains: the uncertainty of evolving a business, taking a romantic relationship to the next level, moving to a new city. Do we resist these painful but crucial experiences, or do we embrace the pain and trust that it's leading us towards our higher self?

Perhaps our pain is physical. We've been having health issues for some time, and now it's clear: it's time to change our diets. We've gathered all the information and we know it's time. It's an uncomfortable realization, but it's for the best—the pain of the change will lead us to better health.

45

So, we hire a dietician or we start with one small change and we sit with the pain of watching our old habits fall away. (The wrong way to go about this would be to exaggerate things and try to make a massive shift all at once. The next thing you know, you're in over your head and you've gone and created unnecessary complexity for yourself, which will surely lead to unnecessary pain.)

Lao-Tzu said that life is a series of natural and spontaneous changes. Don't resist them, that only creates sorrow. Let reality be reality. Let things flow naturally forward. The truth is, life can be painful and wonderful. When a loved one passes away, for example, we feel real grief. If our career ends too soon, the way an athlete's might after an injury, we feel a great sense of loss. When a woman gives birth, she experiences tremendous pain. But if we allow ourselves to experience this natural and healthy pain, we come through it to the other side, having learned valuable lessons and made space for something new and deeper to arrive: a new relationship, a new career, a new child, a new phase of our lives.

My own experience with pain came in the form of health issues. Many years ago, before I began my own transformational work, I used fast food as a way to numb myself to the pain I was feeling. If I felt stressed or victimized, angry or afraid, I'd turn to unhealthy food as a way to make myself feel better—but of course I wasn't feeling better at all. I was simply resisting the real and valid emotions I was feeling and simultaneously creating health problems that would lead me to be hospitalized over and over again. I was close to death, all because I couldn't bear to face my own original pain. I had to get close to death before I could accept that holding on wasn't working for me—only then did I begin to learn how to let go.

Now I've made peace with the world of the uncomfortable, the world I stepped into when I recognized that no 'hamburger meal deal' could fix the pain I was running from. I'm not afraid of being uncomfortable anymore, and that gives me the power to accomplish great things.

So, are we trying to control our pain? Are we trying to block it off? Human beings can go to tremendous lengths to keep from experiencing pain. But sooner or later, we have to go through it, and in the process, we gain a deeper, richer understanding of our own lives.

Pain can be a great teacher.

You see, pain is the doorway to growth, the invitation to heal. Pain can be the great teacher that steers us towards learning our lessons. Aristotle once said, "You don't learn anything without pain." What he meant by this is that if the learning process is easy, it can't be very transformational, and vice versa: if a lesson is deeply painful, it means we have all the more to gain on the other side.

Consider this too: pain can be experienced as someone letting go of us—or us letting go of something. Maybe someone we are in relationship with lets us know it's not working anymore. That's painful, we're being let go of. The relationship is over, and now we have to deal with the feelings that come up in the wake of that loss. Or maybe we become aware that some coping mechanism or some workout routine isn't right for us any longer.

Whatever happens, we're not letting go by choice, we didn't want to be here. Nevertheless, we find ourselves in the world of the uncomfortable, unmoored, searching. Do we self-medicate with our drug of choice, or do we embrace the world of the uncomfortable and the opportunity for growth? It took a near-death experience for me to accept the truth. If I had felt my original pain, I could have saved myself a lot of unnecessary pain. But I didn't address that original pain, so it got louder. It took more work to drown it out, which only led to more complexity, more self-medication, and every type of unconscious resistance I described earlier. I was being stripped.

Being Stripped, or Safe from What?

Novelist Mary Shelley once said, "Nothing is so painful to the human mind as a great and sudden change." Well, to use our own parallel, if we fail to listen to the call to change for long enough, that pain will bring us to our knees, leave us bent and broken and helpless—stripped, one might say—of our ability to resist any longer. Whether it's time to change a career, a lover, or a lifestyle, we can resist for a while and suffer the consequences, but sooner or later we'll reach the point of no return: the point of being stripped. At that point, no matter how hard we try to hold onto that person or that thing, the loss is inevitable, and it's going to be excruciating. Earlier, I referred to this as the brick wall or the Mack truck experience, but the analogy of being stripped works too: if you don't pay attention to the call to change, the change will still come, but you will experience it in a more painful way. I've gone through it myself. As a transformational life and business coach I've facilitated others through it, and I can tell you that nothing is more painful than working through the chaos and devastation of change that has been resisted too long.

The ego is always searching for ways to block us or hold us back from the progress we ought to be making in our lives in an effort to keep us safe. The question we really ought to ask, though, is *"Safe from what?"*

Remember, the primary need of the ego is to protect itself. It convinces us that we need to be kept safe because we live in a dangerous universe. But once we begin to ask what, exactly, the ego is protecting us from, the ego's fear-mongering falls apart and we recognize that the ego is just scared to experience pain. But as we know, no matter how scary pain may be, on the other side of it there is great growth.

When we feel pain, when we worry that perhaps we might be resisting pain, we can ask ourselves, "Is this pain serving a purpose? If this pain were showing me something, what would it be?" In other words, original pain is a message from our higher self—a call to let go, experience the pain, and advance our wellbeing. Perhaps our pain is here to show us that we're holding on too tightly, like a lover who controls her partner out of fear of loss, only to have that partner leave the relationship. In this way, our pain teaches us about things we can't see right away.

I'm suggesting that you learn to connect with your pain instead of running away from it. If you do this, if you step into your painful moments, pain becomes tolerable. Once you begin to work with your pain, you'll know when you need to address it (some pain just needs a doctor's appointment, there's no two ways about it) and when you need to sit with it and see what it has to teach you.

The Activation Principle

If there's something within us that we should be tending to, the Activation Principle is one of the ways our higher self uses to get our attention. Essentially, the Activation Principle states that we're seldom upset for the reason we think.

When someone does something, or says something we don't like, it can activate old, suppressed energy within us. This energy can be repressed emotions such as anger, jealousy, sadness, or fear. It can be repetitive thoughts, images, or memories that haven't been resolved. Once these thoughts or images have been triggered, we can find ourselves becoming fixated or even obsessed with them. Once we know what to look for, we'll notice a measurable emotional charge to this energy.

Once we are activated, the question quickly becomes, what will we do now? Later on, we'll explore different strategies to use when activated. Only one of these strategies requires us to be conscious, whereas the others require little or no consciousness at all to exercise.

I often refer to this activated energy as *Surf's Up!* A good surfer is skilled at riding the waves of the ocean, and over time, they can ride larger waves because they develop the expertise to recognize the velocity and density of the surf; they acquire the inner confidence and proficiency to tackle any wave and ride it out. Just like a surfer, we can learn to recognize when we are activated, how to ride our own activated energy skillfully, and how to successfully release it. Instead of stuffing it or pretending it doesn't exist, we can accept it, flow with it, and transform it.

 **Exercises**

For the exercises below, take some quiet time by yourself. Get still. Picture your higher self.

If you don't have an image of your higher self or your soul just yet, picture the words "Higher Self" on the screen of your mind. Place these words right over your heart. With your journal and pen in hand, read these questions. Go with the first answer that comes to you—write it down. Over time, the answers to these questions will change as you change. Be authentic. Stay in the moment—and breathe!

1) Would it be beneficial for you to surrender to someone or something? To whom or to what?

2) Is there someone or something in your life that you are ready to let go of? Who or what?

3) What's the difference between the original pain in your life and the unnecessary pain? Have you been healing your original pain—or have you been creating more unnecessary pain?

4) On a scale of 1 to 10 (1 being very little, 10 being a lot), how easy is it for you to get activated? Write that number in your journal. What activates you? What does someone have to say—or do—to activate you?

5) *Surf's Up!* Are you activated right now? If yes, if that activated energy had something to say, what would it say? Could you listen? If that energy needed something from you right now, what might that be? Could you give it?

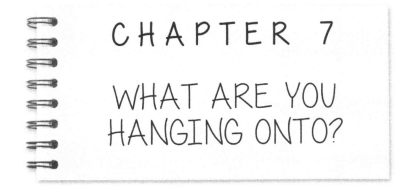

CHAPTER 7

WHAT ARE YOU HANGING ONTO?

Think of the last relationship you let go of. Was it easy? How long did it take? How did you go about it? Were you conscious? Or were you controlling, reactive, maybe even un-conscious? Were you able to surrender? And if you did surrender, at what point did you actually let go?

Let's talk about the power of surrender. Surrender is a powerful act because it comes from the soul-self. When we let go, when we surrender, everything becomes easier. There are still bumps along the way, but those bumps are softer, less painful. When we hold onto things we shouldn't, those bumps are intense, painful—and they needn't be.

The key is choosing to surrender. If a relationship is over, it's over. If someone dear to us has died, they're gone. If a business practice is no longer working, it's no longer working. No amount of struggle will make it work. In fact, struggling will make it worse. It's only when we *surrender to what is* that it all becomes easier.

A client of mine from long ago struggled with surrendering to reality. Her father was very ill, and she was spending all her time with him in the hospital. It became clear that he was going to die. But she couldn't accept it. She tried to control every little thing about the situation, tried to change the reality of it, but nothing made any difference. He was going to die, and her controlling behavior was robbing her of the last precious days with her father. It was only after he died that she recognized her behavior had been harmful to both of them. If she had accepted that he was dying, she could have appreciated their time together more. She beat herself up about it for a while, but eventually she grew from it. She had learned a powerful lesson about the importance of surrendering to what is.

Watch for Messages

The soul, our guides, and our spiritual helpers are constantly sending us messages—they show us billboard ads featuring words ten feet high and notices for movies with themes that resonate in our lives right now, they display significant number sequences, and bring our attention to snippets of the conversations of strangers. When something keeps popping up for us over and over, whether it be a set of numbers or a topic of conversation, it's probably a message from our soul-self, calling us to pay attention. A message could come from other people, from nature, or from our dreams, and its purpose is to remind us that we are loved and supported and that we are being called to change. Those messages ask us to ask ourselves, "What am I supposed to become? What should I let go of? What do I need to embrace? What new thing is making its way into my life?"

The soul speaks quietly, in subtle messages.

The soul will always speak to us quietly in these subtle messages, whereas the ego is never bashful. Famous novelist Erica Jong, author of the wildly successful book, *Fear of Flying,* said that she accepted that fear will always be a part of life, so whenever her ego spoke to her, saying, "Turn back, turn back," she refused and moved forward to embrace change.

Who are You Becoming?

Another way to explore the messages you might be receiving is to ask yourself a series of questions. The first is, "Am I becoming the person I want to be?"

This question has two key aspects. First, as we take a moment to reflect on who we are becoming, we must ask, "Is my current path leading me where I want to go?" We might find that the person we're becoming is not the person we want to be. Maybe we're becoming too soft or sensitive when we want to become stronger and more disciplined. Maybe we're too masculine when we want to become more feminine. Maybe we're becoming controlling. Maybe we're becoming afraid. Maybe we're becoming negative, unhealthy, or broke. Maybe we're becoming angry. Or, maybe we're becoming like someone in our lives that we vowed long ago we would never be like. As we explore this question, we may realize that we're on someone else's path or that we're moving towards a goal we don't really want to achieve. If that's the case, the sooner we can change that path, the better.

The second aspect of the question is, "Who do I want to become? What kind of man do I want to become? What kind of woman do I want to become?" If we find we are headed towards becoming someone we don't want to be, we must take time to reflect. *Who do we want to be?* We can journal about it, we can reach out to dear ones who can support us. We can wrestle with the qualities we want to develop and identify whether or not we're really evolving in that way.

Perhaps we realize we're not the type of parent we want to be. Well, we can ask ourselves, "What kind of parent do I want to become?" Perhaps we're not the spouse or boss or friend we know we want to be. We must ask, "What kind of work do I need to do to be genuine with others?" As we do the work of identifying our areas for improvement, we find ways to manifest them. Soon enough, we'll receive feedback, people will recognize our efforts. They'll tell us that they're inspired by our parenting, our work ethic, or whatever we've been developing.

The ego wants us to become something we will never become. It's a form of distraction. If the ego can distract us from becoming the person we're meant to be, it stays in power and continues to lead us astray. In order to truly become the people we are meant to be, we have to expand our consciousness. But expanding our consciousness, of course, is precisely what our ego is seeking to prevent. The soul wants us to become the true essence of itself, which we can only experience by going through the ego. Meaning, of course, that our soul resides on the other side of our ego.

So how do you manifest the changes necessary to transform into your soul-self? Visualize how the desired change will make you feel! Who do you want to become? Can you visualize that person? Can you see yourself with all the qualities you desire? Once you can, ask yourself, "How does it make me feel?" Really dive into that feeling. Speak the words, "I am a confident, inspiring leader." Or, "I am a beautiful, sensual woman." Or, "I am a self-assured, strong man." Or, "I am an accomplished, diligent student." Or, "I am a connected, conscious parent." By attaching specific feelings to the changes we need to make—and really *feeling those feelings*—we imprint our soul's essence upon the process, we open up our soul, and manifest our best and highest self.

Once we've begun to ask ourselves who we want to become, the question works with us, activating our soul. The soul prompts us to connect with our feelings—and the more we connect to the feeling we desire, the more alive our declaration becomes. Through engaging with our truest feelings, we can manifest our desires and become the person we genuinely want to become.

On Feelings

Speaking of feelings, it's a good practice to examine the current relationship we have with our emotional lives. Our emotions are powerful catalysts in our lives, so it behooves us to check in often with how we are feeling. You can make this check-in part of your daily spiritual practice, sitting quietly and asking for guidance to tap into whatever unconscious or conscious emotions might be motivating your actions. This is how we find our personal power. Our conscious and/or unconscious emotions propel our power. Just as we have relationships with our families, friends, and coworkers, we also have relationships with our emotions.

Most of us don't have a healthy rapport with our feelings. Maybe we're afraid of them, maybe we're so used to numbing ourselves that we don't remember what it's like to feel. This is why there is so much addiction in our modern world—food, shopping, alcohol, drugs, sex, and gambling are just some of the ways we distract ourselves from feeling the lower frequency emotions—fear, shame, guilt, etc.—that are a natural part of life. Some of us are so disconnected that if someone asks how we're doing, we don't know. Disconnecting from our feelings can ruin relationships and destroy careers, because unaddressed emotions get stuck in our bodies and wreak havoc with our systems. If we could just feel our pain or sorrow, grief or anger, the feeling would work itself out and we could move on. It's the act of numbing, distancing, or disconnecting that causes our emotions to remain bottled up inside of us. This is completely unnatural as all our emotional energy knows how to do—all it *wants* to do—is move. Emotion is *energy in motion*.

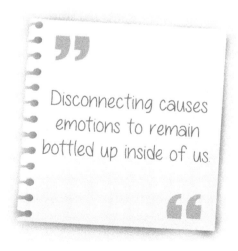

Disconnecting causes emotions to remain bottled up inside of us.

This is why it serves us well to develop a healthy relationship with our feelings. The subconscious is both a chamber for our emotions and the seat of the soul. When we block the channel that allows our emotions to flow freely between the subconscious realms and our world of experience, we also block our connection to our soul-self. The true source of our power lies in connecting to the subconscious—the domain of feeling.

When it comes down to it, either we rule our feelings or they rule us. It's one or the other. By doing transformational work, we can develop a better relationship with our feelings, but doing so requires conscious effort. We must ask ourselves, "Have my feelings been ruling my world?"

Let me offer an example to illustrate.

Imagine your friend comes to you and announces she's going to quit smoking tomorrow. She's elated, and you're elated for her. You know this change is going to make a real difference in her life. But you run into her the next day and she hasn't quit. You ask her why, and she says, "Oh, I had a bad day. I guess it wasn't the right time." This is a key sign that your friend is ruled by her emotions. She allowed her emotions to dictate her behavior. If she were in control of her emotional life, that same bad day wouldn't have derailed her plans. She would have acknowledged that she was stressed or upset and said, "You know what? Quitting smoking is important to me no matter what I'm feeling in this moment."

In the exercises below, I offer a little test. When you do these exercises, you may realize that your feelings seem to have a life of their own—it is as if they are separate entities sharing your physical space. So, you need to decide—who's in charge here, me or my emotions? And, once you decide that you are the governor of your emotions—not the other way around—you can guide your emotions to work for you, not against you. You and your emotions can become a team—working together to create your new, promising future. It feels great!

 **Exercises**

For the exercises below, take some quiet time by yourself. Get still. Picture your higher self.

If you don't have an image of your higher self or your soul just yet, picture the words "Higher Self" on the screen of your mind. Place these words right over your heart. With your journal and pen in hand, read these questions. Go with the first answer that comes to you—write it down. Over time, the answers to these questions will change as you change. Be authentic. Stay in the moment—and breathe!

1) Imagine your soul floating just above you or out in front of you. As you do this, imagine that your soul wants you to know something right now. What might that be?

2) Are you becoming the person you want to become? Who do you want to become?

3) On a scale of 1 to 10 (1 being very little, 10 being a lot), how much have your feelings been running your world? Write this number in your journal. Why did you give yourself this rating or number? Do your feelings control the way you act sometimes? If so, in what way?

4) On a scale of 1 to 10, how protective are you of your feelings? Write this number in your journal. Why did you choose this number?

5) On a scale of 1 to 10, how much have you numbed yourself from your feelings? Write this number in your journal. Why have you numbed yourself?

CHAPTER 8

TO HEAL FOR REAL, WE MUST FEEL FOR REAL

Getting in touch with our feelings does not mean we get lost in them. It is a common misconception that feeling our feelings means drowning in a chaotic swirl of emotions: quite the opposite. When we are connected to our feelings, they pass through us with ease, we remain upright, conscious, and present. Feelings are energy, and energy wants to move.

In their uninhibited state, feelings flow naturally. We learn from them and respect them without fearing or forcing them. Perhaps, for example, we used to suffer from unbridled anger, but when we let it go, the anger flowed through us and we moved on in a matter of minutes. To heal for real, we must feel for real.

We don't have to get lost in our feelings or dramatize them around others in order to *feel* feelings. Lower-frequency feelings such as anger, sadness, or grief hold energy that wants to be released—they are not beneficial when suppressed. Holding onto negative feelings for an extended time creates unnecessary problems in life. *Feeling* is a skill set anybody can learn. Once we learn how to feel consciously, we can respond to our emotions as they arise and the feelings in and of themselves can move quickly. Many times, as feelings move through us, they provide great insight through which we can see our world differently—and when this happens, everything changes.

To heal for real, we must feel for real, and to feel for real, we must give ourselves permission to feel our emotions fully. This brings two questions into awareness: "Are we in control of our feelings?" and "Are our feelings controlling us?" As we have seen, a person controlled by their feelings declares excitedly what they're going to do, recognizing it's the right thing. However, the next day, they're feeling down, and they don't get started. After a few more days, they still don't *feel* like doing something new so, again, they don't get started.

On the other hand, a person in control of their feelings declares excitedly what they're going to do, recognizing it's the right thing. The next day they're feeling down, but they *do* get started. After a few more days, even though they still don't feel like doing the new thing, they continue to do it anyway. They don't shut their feelings down. They've learned either how to enter into a conscious agreement with whatever it is they're feeling, understanding that they will return and work with the feelings later, or they've developed the skill and consciousness to work through their feelings while they do what they set out to do.

Someone in control of their feelings experiences life differently than someone whose feelings control them. Every person genuine in their intent to do something new experiences days when they don't want to do it, especially at the beginning. Even for a person in control of their feelings, it's an up and down process: one day they feel like it, the next day, they don't. But they have a conscious relationship to their feelings and healthy control of their emotional world, so they get things done.

Those who are controlled by their feelings are frustrated by the transformational process; their choices are based on how and/or what they're feeling here and now, not on doing the right thing here and now. This is why developing a healthy relationship with our feelings by becoming conscious of them can change everything for the better—forever.

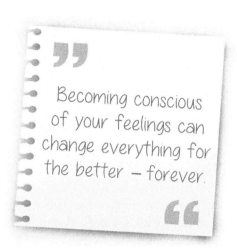

Becoming conscious of your feelings can change everything for the better – forever.

The key to becoming conscious of your relationship with your feelings is to consider your answers to the questions asked earlier. Ask yourself these questions again, and this time, rate your answer on a scale of 1 to 10 (1 being very little and 10 being a lot). Then, ask yourself, "Why did I give myself that rating?"

"How much have your feelings have been ruling your world?" "How much have your feelings been controlling your behavior?" "How protective or guarded are you of your feelings?" "How much have you numbed out your ability to feel?"

This is a good exercise to record in your journal—check in with yourself—where are you really at in your relationship to your feelings? Take charge! You may be surprised when you first realize, "Oh my gosh! I can actually create my life the way I genuinely want it to be!"

Dealing with Feelings

What do you do when feelings come up? What primary strategy do you use to deal with your feelings? We all have a strategy and it's an important part of our overall wellbeing. In order to change our lives moving forward, it's important to recognize the strategy we've been using, because it may no longer be helpful.

The "Three S's system" is a great process for managing your feelings. In this model, the first S is for *spirit* or *spirituality*, getting in touch with your soul; the second S is for *structure*, finding the right kind of support; and the third S is for *strategy*, incorporating a methodology or transformational system to help you control your emotions. We'll cover the three S's later in the section called "Triad for Transformation," but here, we'll cover a few helpful aspects of the third S, *strategy*, so you can discover which one you are employing in your life right now—and then you can decide whether or not you need to change it up for a new approach that will help you become your true and best self.

There are seven main strategies we use both consciously and unconsciously when dealing with feelings. Which strategy are you using to keep your emotions in check?

Stuff 'Em

I've called the first strategy "Stuff 'Em." What does it look like to Stuff 'Em? Well, something has happened and you are angry, sad, grieving, fearful, etc. The next thing you know, your automatic strategy (which you may be unconscious of) starts and you "stuff" your feelings. How? The most common way is through eating. Remember, the ego works through the modality of falsehood—it can convince us, for example, that we're hungry for something, when we're not hungry for that at all. We might do it unconsciously, but the next thing we know, we're reaching for a box of candies, a pizza, or a bag of potato chips. We're literally stuffing the feelings with food.

There are other ways we can stuff as well. We stuff feelings through becoming a workaholic—I'm not saying we shouldn't work a lot, especially those who are passionate about work—however, if work is our way of "stuffing," then that's a sure sign that we're being called to change.

Question your stuffing behaviors—ask yourself, "What's going on?" "Do I have to have another drink (or candy, or chips, etc.)?" Or, more specifically, "*Why* am I doing this? Do I just want to enjoy a drink, because it's the right time of day? Or is something up for me feeling-wise and I'm repressing it, driving it back deep within me?"

Avoid 'Em

The second strategy we use when dealing with feelings is to "Avoid 'Em." How? We create a distraction. Some people create a To Do list. If we're engaging in an activity in order to avoid a feeling, it ends up getting re-repressed; it gets re-buried within our subconscious mind. We might quickly change the subject as the conversation with someone shifts towards a heated issue. Or, because of what comes up for us when we enter an uncomfortable conversation, we might avoid someone, run away, retreat, or perhaps become crazy-busy—all with the intent of sidestepping an uncomfortable situation. A person who continually uses this strategy—or any of the first five strategies, actually—eventually gets jammed up with feelings and, sooner or later, they get overwhelmed.

Power 'Em   *for control*

I sometimes refer to the third strategy as "Power 'Em," as in "power them up." A person who Powers 'Em feeds power to their rising emotions or activated energy. When they do this, the feeling or the activated energy becomes stronger. They can blow things out of proportion, making situations in their lives bigger than what they really are. This is a protection strategy; this person has a pattern of giving their power away to someone or something. Where is this power-depletion rooted? It's rooted in this person's tendency to give their power away—to others, to the words of others, or to their own feelings—all because they are afraid of the world of emotions. Say, for example, this person feels angry. In giving power to the anger, they open themselves up to becoming overwhelmed because they mismanage the anger. When the anger isn't processed correctly, it becomes intense. The feeling spins out of control because they empower it, and in the moment, they may say or do something they might be sorry for later. The same thing may happen in a conversation with a coworker or spouse, whereby one person gives power to the emotion or to the words of another—and then ends up feeling depleted, like, "What just happened?" Another way this strategy might show itself is when someone says something negative or even mean to us. If their words hurt, it might be because we're "powering up" their words, or giving our power away.

63

We might hear ourselves saying things like, "You hurt my feelings." So, keep in mind that this Power 'Em strategy won't work for you—ever. It entails giving feelings power, and regardless of whose feeling is fueled, Power 'Em never improves any situation. In fact, inevitably it ends with someone shutting down—a wedge is driven between two people, or a wall goes up between them. The two people are no longer as open—to themselves or to one another—as they once were.

Worship 'Em

The fourth strategy is to "Worship 'Em." Some people give their feelings supreme power, and by doing this, they protect themselves from having to deal with their feelings and ultimately, to confront them. This person will not let go of their feelings because everything has become focused around them; they allow their feelings to guide their actions. We saw this "Worship 'Em" strategy at play earlier, in the example of a friend who wants to quit smoking, but never does. Some people worship their feelings; whatever they are feeling, they do. If they don't feel like following through on something they said they were going to do, they don't do it. It's only about doing the things that are matched to what they are feeling in the moment, rather than doing the thing that is right for them to be doing in the moment. But when their feelings slide into the lower frequency vibrations of sadness, grief, fear, etc., they get stuck. They sabotage themselves and hold themselves back.

Actually, any of these strategies ultimately hold us back, but this is the more obvious one—any forward movement that you might create through good intentions comes to an almost immediate halt when you utilize the "Worship 'Em" strategy.

Act 'Em

The fifth strategy is to act out on our feelings because we don't want to embrace them, we want to get rid of them. In this strategy, for example, say we have a negative or positive feeling towards someone and, in order to get rid of the feeling, we express it out loud the first chance we get. We discover, however, that acting in this way can backfire—producing even more unnecessary pain and resistance. Perhaps the person we're expressing our feelings to (whether our feelings are positive or negative), isn't open to receiving them just yet. As mentioned with the Worship 'Em strategy, with Act 'Em, we can let our feelings rule us. For example, if we're feeling negative, we let someone else know by acting out our negative feelings on them. When we're using the Act 'Em strategy, our choices are often based on how we *feel*, not on doing the things that resolve a situation or help us to move forward in our life.

Project 'Em   my main stragity

The sixth strategy is "Project 'Em." In this strategy, when a person has feelings they don't want to deal with in a conscious, responsible way, they protect themselves by projecting their feelings onto another person. They believe either that the other person is the cause of their feelings or that the other person feels their feelings. Sometimes, the other person will say, "No. You keep saying I feel this way but I don't. Here's how I'm really feeling." And they argue—leading to more improperly expressed or unresolved feelings—and around it goes. For example, say someone has a fear of being made wrong and uses this strategy to protect themselves from feeling wrong. They can project their fear onto someone else by making that other person wrong for something they did—or even didn't do.

Again, these six of the seven strategies all lead to the same place: they keep us safe from experiencing or confronting our feelings. That's what we're trying to protect ourselves from—we never want to feel this stuff again. The challenge is, as long as this stuff is inside of us, it'll keep making itself known until we get what's going on: we've buried our feelings. They keep bubbling to the surface and as they do, we launch into one of these six strategies: stuffing, avoiding, powering, worshiping, acting, or projecting. We do one of these six until we become conscious that "this is what I'm doing." *That realization* changes everything for the better because by declaring this, we take responsibility for our own feelings—which brings us to Strategy number seven.

Clear 'Em

This seventh strategy is for true transformation seekers—"Clear 'Em." This strategy, propounded by many wonderful teachers, helps you to clear out suppressed emotional material. This strategy is about choosing to clear emotions as soon as feelings arise (regardless of what those feelings are) and helping them to move on. Instead of acting on one of the other strategies, every time we choose to clear, we're moving emotional energy. That's all the energy wants: to move, to be released. Emotions are at the root of our core issues and the better we get at clearing them, the more other buried feelings begin to surface, unwind, and move. As we clear, we bring more consciousness to our core issues, which empowers us to deal with them responsibly. So, as we peel away layers of emotional material, and clear them, we resolve our issues for good—and we heal, for good.

Time Heals

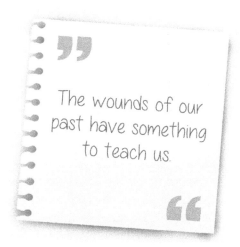

The wounds of our past have something to teach us.

We've all heard it: time heals everything. But does it really? Is it that simple? Of course not. For the most part, it simply doesn't work. Why? Because to heal our past, more than likely, there is something rooted in repressed emotions that we ought to be processing. If we're waiting for time to pass with the hopes that suppressed feelings will go away, we will not heal. Waiting for our healing to come could be one of the tricks of the ego. The wounds of our past have something to teach us and if this teaching is not integrated into our day-to-day reality, we'll continue to be held back by our painful past experiences. Real, positive, lasting change is not created by the passage of time, but by the transformation of consciousness.

In his book, *Letting Go*, Dr. David Hawkins emphasizes that "...the letting go of negative feelings is the undoing of the ego, which will be resistant at every turn." He goes on to say, "...let the resistance be there, but don't resist the resistance."

You see, if we resist our resistance, it only makes the ego stronger—for that which we oppose becomes stronger. And if the ego can trick us into resisting the resistance, we will never process our old, suppressed emotions and our past, painful experiences.

Yet as we allow our feelings and emotions to come up over time, and we clear them as our primary strategy, a transformation of consciousness takes place within us that creates enduring change. By letting go of our resistance to change, and developing the transformational practice of clearing our emotional blockages as they arise, we get time on our side and align with the natural, healing rhythms of nature. And as we do this, everything changes for the better forever.

Are You Trying to Change the Past?

Hoping to change the past is another form of unconscious resistance. The truth is, we can't change the past. However, we can change how we feel about the past and that can change our trajectory. You see, holding down old emotions keeps the whole past experience in play.

Psychoanalyst Carl Jung said it this way: *What we resist, persists*. If I'm resisting my old, suppressed feelings and/or emotions, they will persist. As they persist, they grow stronger. It's the transformation of lower-frequency consciousness—our old, suppressed, feeling-oriented material from past experiences—that creates real change.

Exercises

For the exercises below, take some quiet time by yourself. Get still. Picture your higher self.

If you don't have an image of your higher self or your soul just yet, picture the words "Higher Self" on the screen of your mind. Place these words right over your heart. With your journal and pen in hand, read these questions. Go with the first answer that comes to you—write it down. Over time, the answers to these questions will change as you change. Be authentic. Stay in the moment—and breathe!

1) Are you in control of your feelings, or have your feelings been controlling you? If you control your feelings, how do you control them? If your feelings control you, how do they do so?
tantrums yelling anger, worry

2) Which strategy (as in *Project 'Em*, *Worship 'Em*, etc.) have you been using most when it comes to your feelings? Have you used a second or third strategy as well? Which one(s)? What situation, person, etc. can motivate you to use these strategies?

3) On a scale of 1 to 10 (1 being very little, 10 being a lot), how often do you clear your emotional energy? Write this number in your journal. Explain how you clear your emotional energy.
2 times a day

4) On a scale of 1 to 10, how strong has your resistance been to change? Write this number in your journal. How do you show up when you are resisting? *Controlling.*
5

5) What strategy did you use today? Was there a need influencing your choice of that strategy? Did you clear something today? If so, what?

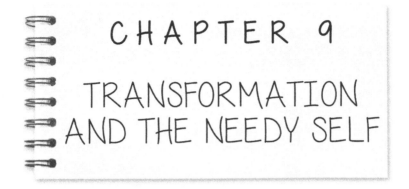

CHAPTER 9

TRANSFORMATION AND THE NEEDY SELF

We can all relate to resisting change, dealing with repressed emotions, and running away from experiencing the pain that life can dole out. But when we resist, repress, or run away, instead of facing life's problems and predicaments, we miss the opportunity for personal growth that is held inside of them. After all, we're all here to transform ourselves, ready or not, so we may as well get started!

There are three paths to transformation, and seven core issues that can help us meet life's challenges head on.

Three Paths to Transformation

Everyone and everything is in a constant state of change; it's up to us to decide whether we resist or embrace its transformative power. True personal transformation begins when we accept that our purpose is to change some aspect of ourselves.

There are three ways to do transformational work: through process work, through life experience, and through receiving higher teachings. Each path begins at a different point, but all authentic transformational teachers touch upon each path at some point. In the end, it doesn't matter how you do the work, it matters only that the work is accomplished.

On the first path, the path of *process*, transformational seekers realize that something in their life is amiss and they take steps to correct it. They see the value of processing their own emotional energy and doing the inner work. As they progress, they encounter life-changing experiences and higher teaching mentors, but they begin their work through the simple act of *deciding to make a change*.

The second path, the path of *experience*, is the method of those who begin their transformational work with a wake-up call. Something shakes them loose from their daily life—an accident, a health scare, the sudden end of a relationship. Whatever the catalyst, this seeker realizes that their life needs to change. It can be scary or unsettling to experience such an abrupt worldview change, but this individual is set on a path to connecting with their soul-self—and once they strike out on this journey, there is no turning back.

The third path is for those who encounter some *higher teaching* along their life's journey. This teaching could be a holy book, a transformational teacher or life coach, a powerful piece of writing, or a body of wisdom—however they come across it, they become inspired to seek transformation in some area of their life.

My transformational journey began with the path of *experience*. It was many years ago; a friend recommended that I go to a healer about some pain I was experiencing. As soon as I walked into the healer's office, I felt a powerful sense of security, but I was also anxious. We talked, then he took me into a treatment room, began his adjustment, and immediately I felt a strange sensation filling me. At first I was curious, then afraid: I had never felt anything like it. I felt like I was losing control of my body. I struggled with a control issue at the time and I felt powerless—out of control in a terrifying way. My breathing became shallow, my whole body tingled with fear. Typically, sessions with this healer last forty-five minutes to an hour, but that day I spent five hours working through my fear and pain with him. That session was a wake-up call, the event that inspired me to begin my own transformational journey.

Again, it doesn't matter where we start, what matters is that we keep going. It's not easy. There were many times during the early years of my journey when I wanted desperately to abandon my path. I felt lost, confused, I couldn't see where all this work was taking me. But my body knew I had to keep going. As the years passed and I began to coach others, I watched them struggle with confusion and doubt too. The hardest part of transformational work is that while we're in it, it can be hard to see the other side. Transformational work never really ends—but the hard parts do end. Little by little we continue, because our divine nature is always to be expanding and growing. We know that all people are called to change, but most people resist. They hold themselves back, preventing their souls from expanding and reaching their fullest potential.

When the World Closes In

Our souls are meant to be expanding constantly, but sometimes we feel like the world is closing in. If you feel trapped or stuck, it means that big change is knocking on your door. It could be personal, professional, financial, spiritual, emotional, or mental, but change is coming: you just can't see it yet. If you feel this way, there are options. You can seek help from a transformational life coach or another professional—someone who can help you understand what's causing your suffering. I encourage you to seek help, but I also suggest that part of your suffering comes from resistance. Your ego is influencing you to hang onto destructive relationships, to avoid new opportunities, to run away from what scares you, to maintain the status quo even when the status quo is unpleasant. The first step towards change is acknowledging that something is wrong. So, when you know you're in pain, you're already on your way to transformation!

The Seven Core Issues

As we do our transformational work, we must dig down into our subconscious and identify the core issues that hold us back. In my experience, there are seven core issues, major problems that afflict the vast majority of people I've worked with. Most of us have at least one primary core issue, many of us will have a secondary issue or multiple issues that bolster the main one. Our issues have been with us for most of our lives, and they influence everything we do. Whether we are aware of them or not (and probably we are unaware of them), our core issues motivate us to make poor choices and behave badly towards those we love. These issues intertwine like the tangled branches of a thicket, holding us back from any real growth. Let us examine these core issues so that we can begin to release them and move on.

Control Issues, Power Issues

As discussed, there is a real difference between *having control* and *being controlling*. There is a way to have a healthy degree of control in our lives, but like all core issues, control issues come from a deep-seated, unaddressed need to protect ourselves from pain. Our need to be in control manifests in us misusing power, manipulating those around us, or bullying others. Someone with a control issue always has to have the last word.

Control issues often come up in a business context, so I distinguish between "inspiring leaders" and "controlling leaders." Inspiring leaders empower their workers to grow and thrive; controlling leaders yell, make unrealistic demands, and oppress their workers.

Let's distinguish between a boss who leads through egoic control and someone who leads through authentic, disciplined, and inspiring leadership. For example, imagine the head of a corporation who gets some bad news from an employee. An egoic leader, someone who pursues leadership as a form of control or an expression of self-centeredness, would lash out, because the bad news would be perceived as a threat to her authority. But a true, inspiring leader, someone who approaches her position as a call to service, would view the bad news as an opportunity for growth, and would thank the employee for her honesty and hard work. This individual is connected to her soul-self, wants to make a difference, and has no time for or interest in self-aggrandizement.

The differing approaches employed by inspiring and controlling bosses can have drastic effects on workplace morale, and on everything from productivity to office stress levels to employee turnover. Even as the egoic, controlling person works to control everything, things just spiral further out of control. True, soulful, and inspiring leaders, on the other hand, are authentically humble. They are inspired by those around them, so they will always seek to highlight the good work of others—and in this way, they get their employees on side and get things done.

Safety Issues, Protection Issues

If we have an issue about feeling safe, we live in a state of constant insecurity, feeling as though there's danger at every turn. Of course, a true sense of security comes from within, but when we have a safety issue, we want to wrap ourselves in protective clothing so we'll never get hurt. But as I said, true transformational work is scary. It's not until we can feel secure within ourselves that we can get down to real transformational work.

I see this come up when I lead transformational seminars that last three or more days, long enough for people to undergo some change. Over days, people begin to feel safer and they drop their barriers—so they progress further than they could have otherwise. It's amazing to witness.

A safety issue can make us feel like it's the end of the world, even when nothing is actually happening. When this issue gets triggered, it sends us into a panic; we come out swinging. Perhaps we'll lash out with our words, or, if the safety issue is deeply lodged within us, we'll even lash out with our fists. The safety issue runs the show; we feel vulnerable, scared, and we act out violently. We're trying to feel safe, but our actions make us feel less safe, so the vicious cycle continues.

Commitment Issues, Trust Issues

Most of us know what it's like to have someone in our corner, fully committed to our growth and evolution. Some people have experienced the power of committing to another's growth, and/or to their own growth. Yet, if we have commitment issues, we don't know what this feels like, so growing and evolving can be excruciatingly painful. And, if we have trouble committing, we likely have trouble trusting as well. Either we trust no one or we place our trust in the wrong people. When we have a trust issue, often we can't see clearly. Perhaps, for example, we do not trust financial opportunities that come our way— or we place our trust in a faulty opportunity—which leads to a further lack of trust. Lack of trust can lead to allowing our emotions to rule our actions—and that in turn can lead to further pain and confusion. Sometimes things seem so difficult we may ask, "How did I get here?" If our commitment issue is deep enough, doing our best means having only one foot in anything we do.

⭐ Confidence Issues, Value and Worth Issues

How much do you like yourself? The mark of a person who possesses high self-esteem is someone who likes themselves. If, for example, I like myself, it becomes easy for me to like others as well. Partly this is because my self-esteem attracts people into my life that are genuinely likeable, and partly it is because when I like myself, I try new things and meet new people who are on the same 'wavelength.' As I become victorious in mastering new things and making new friends, I build inner confidence.

But if a lack of self-esteem is one of my issues, then I will struggle with finding likable qualities in myself as well as in others. When I don't like myself, I feel uncomfortable in my own skin and I resist trying new things in my life. For example, one effect of low self-esteem can be the habit or behavioral pattern of procrastination. We procrastinate when we lack confidence or certainty inside ourselves—because we're afraid of what the result of our efforts and actions would say to everyone in our outer world. Will someone see that I'm really not good enough or that I'm not perfect?

Similarly, when we don't know our *true value*, we may try to make ourselves look like more than we are (or like less than we are), or we'll try to convince the person we're with that their value is of little importance to us. If we have an issue with our value, we also have an issue with our worth. It's beautiful to feel worthy, but that powerful feeling can never come from the panicked neediness of a worth issue.

When we struggle with a worth issue, the key word is "enough." There's never a pause point. It feels constantly like we're not good enough, like there will never be enough money, enough love, enough attention, enough energy, enough time. If we get a promotion, it's not enough: we're always striving for the next level of career advancement. We're always working to be one step better, to get one more thing; we don't stop to appreciate what we have. The worth issue burns us out, it makes us work, work, work, achieve more, be better—it never allows us the luxury of enjoying the *now*.

Worth issues manifest in every area of our lives, but let us examine it in the context of a romantic relationship. If we feel unworthy, at some point we will sabotage our relationship, turning our worth issue into a self-fulfilling prophecy. We'll distance ourselves from our loved one, believing that we're unworthy of love. But it's our act of distancing that ruins the relationship, not our essential worth.

When we feel unworthy, we are likely to push away the best things in life, falsely believing that we don't deserve them. This will likely lead to depression. It's only when we discover and connect with the true value of our soul that we begin to feel worthy again—worthy of love, of respect, and of success. Only then can we climb out of that dark sadness and appreciate what we have without pushing it away. When that happens, we can embrace the good in our lives, and that is a sure sign that a worth issue is resolving.

Validation Issues, Acceptance Issues

It is marvelous to feel validated and accepted. It's great to be told that you did a good job or that you're appreciated for your contributions, it helps you to thrive as a human being. But when the need to be affirmed comes from a hungry, needy place, there can never be enough validation. When we struggle with a validation issue, we're always reaching for one more bit of praise. The funny thing about having a validation issue is that when it's in the driver's seat, we seem to put ourselves in situations where we'll never be accepted. The simple truth is that no one can validate us if we don't believe we're worthy of validation. So, we keep seeking that sweet salve of praise, knowing deep down that it won't fix the craving inside. Around and around we go, looking for the next validation. We're not actually progressing: we're just trying to do whatever will look good so that someone gives us praise. The ego gets in there, convinces us we're making progress, but all we're doing is spinning in place, going nowhere. The only way off the hamster wheel is self-acceptance, coming to know in a deep, true way that we are worthy of praise, simply for being who we are.

Entrepreneurs frequently suffer from the validation issue. Many people start their own business to get that sense of validation. They set up shop and only then do they realize that their need to be validated hasn't been soothed at all, so they make business choices designed to gain validation, even if it doesn't make sense for the business. So, many people start businesses—but only some people mature into fully responsible and genuine business leaders.

Significance Issues, Identity Issues

People who suffer from identity issues don't have a true sense of themselves. They put on acts and try on personalities because they have no sense of the type of person they're meant to be. Of course, this creates a whole maze of other issues. They emulate other people, and imitate people they admire, but because they're motivated by a sense of confusion, they often emulate people who may not be the best role models—which only leads them further from their true path. If they live this way for five years, ten years, twenty years, the maze they create becomes thick and they produce extreme, unnecessary pain for themselves.

The beautiful thing is, the path to resolving an identity issue will also resolve the maze of confusion we've built. We don't need an "Aha!" moment, we don't need to wake up one morning and suddenly know exactly who we are. We simply have to start asking ourselves questions about our core truths. As we figure out what we believe in, what we want, and how we ought to be living, we accept that we're here on purpose. We realize that our life has value in and of itself—not in the way the ego would have us believe but in the deeper, truer way of the soul. We've all come here to add value to the lives of others. Recognizing this is incredibly freeing, and we begin to have space to become our true selves once again.

Separation Issues, Isolation Issues

Individuals who suffer from separation issues and isolation have often experienced a point in their early lives where they separated—knowingly or unknowingly—from some part of themselves. Perhaps they rejected a talent or a gift as 'not being good enough' or perhaps they disconnected from their masculine or feminine side. Perhaps issues of survival forced them to detach from their soul-self. When this early sense of separation occurs, there can be a tendency for an individual to isolate as a way to keep from feeling the pain of separation. Over time, not only can this isolation become very painful, it can also keep us from engaging with those we are meant to be in relationship with and doing what we are meant to be doing. Thus, separation and isolation issues are serious roadblocks to the fulfillment of one's life purpose. Overcoming them often means confronting and resolving each of the core issues on this list of seven. But once the decision is made to rise to this challenge— watch this individual soar!

Primary and Secondary Core Issues

Until we begin our transformational journey, we all struggle with one or more of these core issues. It can be useful to imagine them as primary and secondary issues. Perhaps, for example, our worth issue is the strongest of our core issues, the one that causes us the deepest suffering. But, secondary to the worth issue is an identity issue—we not only feel unworthy of love, we don't know who we are. Or, perhaps we have a primary worth issue and a secondary safety issue, which manifests as unworthy feelings that trigger a terrifying sense of insecurity, leading us to act out. In this way, our core issues construct a maze of actions and reactions, leading us further away from our true path.

The Needy Self

The needy self is both the source of and the consequence of resistance. In a vicious cycle of craving and resisting, the needy self keeps the soul-self at bay. The soul-self, on the other hand, has genuine needs that are there to remind us of what it is we're to be moving towards. For example, the soul might need to learn something specific to enable its consciousness to grow and expand here in the physical world. Or, the soul-self might need to contribute something significant to someone or to some cause that would contribute to the resolution of its karma. (We'll explore this subject deeply in the next book of our transformational trilogy, *Transform Your Destiny*.)

The needy self is the part of the ego that influences us to try to get something, or push on something, or keep us in the energetic loop of always wanting something. The whole design of the needy self is to keep us in resistance to its tricks and it's the number one way in which the ego can—and will, if we're not aware—hold us back from moving forward in our lives.

Think, for example, of someone you know who has become very needy. All you have to do is hang out with this person for a while and you get turned off. You need a break; their energy is too heavy. You could say that this person has "pushed you away." As noted, resistance, at its core, is a pushing energy.

As the ego hides behind the needy self, it masks our core issues and becomes stronger over time. However, once we become aware of the needy self and how it reinforces our core issues, we can completely resolve them. As we explored previously, core issues drive us to pursue real, important needs from a place of insecurity and fear, from a needy, seeking energy that can never be satisfied. Like a dog chasing its tail, we can strive forever and never be satiated. We know this isn't productive, and that good things come to us when we let go, surrender, and move on, not when we anxiously pursue the same base needs. We must let go of our constant seeking, our pushing and trying; we must stop expending energy pointlessly. And, in order to do that, we must understand exactly what it is we are so desperate to attain.

The ego masks our core issues and becomes stronger over time.

In my work, I have identified more than 300 needs that spring from the seven core issues, but I will present a dozen or so here so you can begin to identify what needs might be driving you.

There's the need *to be right*. We've all been around this person: they're insufferable. It doesn't matter what the truth is, they'll keep pushing on the subject until the other person admits they're wrong. When someone has a strong need to be right, they would rather be right than happy.

There's the need *to be noticed*. If I pursue the need to be noticed in this needy, hungry way, I'll never get the kind of attention I want. I'll act out in strange ways, and if people do notice me, it won't be in a good way. If I'm operating out of a need to be noticed, it's almost impossible for others to genuinely notice me. I'm pushing too hard, pushing on the other person to notice me, so I stay in the energetic loop of wanting but never receiving.

There's the need *to save others*, even when those others demonstrate no desire to be saved. If we're driven by the need to be a savior, for example, we won't listen to someone telling us to leave them alone. We'll try even harder to save or fix them—even at the risk of driving a wedge between ourselves and the person we care for.

There's the need *to be important*. This might manifest in a family setting whereby one person always has the last word, always talks the loudest, making the rest of the family feel like they're stuck in the "loud one's" orbit. Or, perhaps a business leader is driven by this need: he or she runs around, desperately trying to be important, but that's an easy act to see through and a surefire way to not be chosen for important projects. This kind of behavior comes when we feel unimportant or unvalued on the inside; no official title or recognition can soothe our need to feel important.

There's the need *to be needed*. This person will seek out other people and care for them in a way that robs them of their own independence, making them feel choked by a misplaced sense of care. When you are in a relationship with this type of person, it can seem like you need them but it's probably the other way around—they need you.

There's the need *to figure it out*. Solving problems is a great thing—just look at the scientific community—but many people suffer from a needy energy that makes them endlessly, futilely pursue solutions to problems that might never be solved. This can cause tremendous stress as that individual's abilities to calm down and to relax are completely dependent on them "figuring it out." But what if that takes a long time?

There's the need *to be heard*. Being heard is fantastic: it makes us feel like we belong, like we are connected. But when we have a strong need to be heard, we push the connection away. No matter how hard we try, we will never be heard if we approach it from the perspective of an unresolved need.

There's the need *to please*. It's wonderful to make other people happy, but if the energy we dedicate to pleasing others comes from a place of wounded need, it's not going to work. If we only feel our value when others allow us to please them, it can turn people off. It's too much because it's not coming from an authentic place.

There's the need *to be liked*. When we need to be liked, everything we say and do comes not from our soul-self, or from our genuine personality, but from a lower desire to make people like us. Only when we heal and transform our needy self can we act in a way that will motivate others to like us. When we genuinely like ourselves, it makes it a lot easier for others to like us.

There's the need *to be concerned*. It's good to be concerned about family and friends and work, but when we need desperately to worry about things, we throw our lives out of balance. We all know someone who worries all the time, no matter how good their life is. That's a needy energy and it accomplishes nothing.

There's the need *to play it safe*. If we suffer from this need, we'll hold ourselves back from real growth because it's scary outside of our comfort zone. We see this in people who have been single for a long time: they're scared to pursue love because they're afraid of getting hurt.

There's the need *to prove something to someone*, which is ultimately just a need to prove something to yourself. Needing to prove that you're a good friend or good mate might turn off your friend or mate eventually or even push them away.

Predictably, this need is associated with having a worth issue. If our issue is hooked into others, we feel our worth or importance only when they do what we want them to do. When they don't do what we want them to do, we get upset, we feel unworthy, unimportant. If this issue is hooked into what we do (as in our work or what we do for others), we only feel worthy when we're doing that. If we're still trying to prove ourselves, it's because we haven't claimed our true worth or value yet.

There's the need *for attention*. This need is often exhibited by individuals who have significance or identity issues. Because they don't know who they are, the way they dress, act, or show up is designed to get attention. But often, their strategy backfires, and they draw *negative* attention.

There's the need for *respect*. Once again, it's not that we shouldn't have respect. However, genuine respect is usually earned, not given. For example, imagine a parent who forces their child to give them respect because of their own esteem or confidence issue. Once their child moves into adult life, they no longer respect the parent. Similarly, if I need you to respect me and I push myself on you, I'll push your respect away.

Lastly, there's the need to be *positional*. Of course, there are times in life when it's important to take a position—whether it's standing up for yourself or supporting someone else. That's different, however, than when someone has a needy positional energy. This person refuses to let go of the way they see things, they have a stubborn streak and a control or power issue. Needy positional energy can literally push someone or something that an individual considers valuable right out of their lives. When an individual's positional neediness is strong, they may even experience a problem with circulation, whereby they push so hard to get their way that their skin goes pale or white. I have witnessed this personally in some of my students, and it is not healthy.

As we learn to bring our attention and awareness to needs that are currently influencing our lives, we can resolve and let go of them. So, ask yourself, "What need is dominating my actions and activities today?" If, for example, you need to be liked, ask yourself, "On a scale of 1 to 10, how strong is my need to be liked?" Similarly, if you need to please others, ask yourself, "How strong is my need to please?" Bringing your neediness into conscious awareness foils the ego and helps you to resolve and change. After all, the whole design of the needy self is to create different ways to keep us in unconscious resistance. By holding onto that needy energy, we weaken over time. By releasing it, we become strong and empowered.

So, check in with yourself on a regular basis. If you find yourself being insensitive, defensive, or protective; mean, bossy, or demanding; withdrawn, negative, or pushy; selfish, overly critical, or callous; ask yourself, "What need do I have right now that is not being met? Is my need for control, respect, protection, validation, significance, or value influencing me right now? How has the situation I am in right now activated that need? Do I want to continue allowing my need to run the show? If not, how can I release my attachment to this need?"

The truth is, everyone has significance and is significant. If we're struggling, however, to feel our significance in the world, we may find ourselves pushing or trying, needing to prove our worthiness to others because we haven't yet discovered and claimed our true worth.

There are many more needs than I have listed here, but these are some ways you can begin to dial in on your needy self and discover how it may be influencing your behavior. Whatever need is ruling your life, as you examine the strength of that need, you begin to let go of it. You can ask yourself, "If an inner need is driving me, what is it? Is it the need to be right? The need to be liked? The need to play it safe?" Whatever answer feels true, then ask, "If I measured this need's level of strength, on a scale of 1-10, how strong is that need in my life?"

Put this to the test in your own life: What does it look like when you're resisting someone or something? In the moment, are you looking for a distraction...something to distract you from what you really ought to be doing?

- Is there something or someone you're currently avoiding?

- Are you exaggerating something in your life right now?

- Are you being manipulative with someone or something?

- Are you being reactive? If so, to whom or to what are you reacting? What is it about them or that thing that you're reacting to?

Over the course of my career, I've come to realize that needs are like weeds in the garden of our consciousness—and, more specifically, our subconscious. Weeds are natural, but a good gardener knows that if weeds go unchecked, they'll suffocate the beautiful flowers. The same is true of our needs. It is natural and good to have needs, but if we let them run rampant, they'll choke out what is good in our lives.

As we become conscious of the needs that drive us, we can heal and resolve the issues that lie underneath them. Only then can we begin to build better relationships, better businesses, and better lives.

 **Exercises**

For the exercises below, take some quiet time by yourself. Get still. Picture your higher self.

If you don't have an image of your higher self or your soul just yet, picture the words "Higher Self" on the screen of your mind. Place these words right over your heart. With your journal and pen in hand, read these questions. Go with the first answer that comes to you—write it down. Over time, the answers to these questions will change as you change. Be authentic. Stay in the moment—and breathe!

1) Which one of the three paths to transformation speaks to you? What has your experience with the other two paths been? Describe your last transformational experience.

2) Is there something wrong in your life, or with the way you've been living it? What? How? What might it feel like to change these things?

3) Which of the seven core issues resonates most with you? Does that core issue show up more in your personal life, your professional life, or both? And, when it does show up, what have you noticed?

4) Awareness is Power! Each morning, think of the day that lies ahead of you. As you do, notice if there is a need influencing the theme or quality of your day (e.g. a need to look good, a need for attention, or a need for something else). Write down that need. Then, whatever you write, ask yourself, "Can I just let go of this need?" Journal about that. Remember, it's not that we shouldn't receive attention or look good, etc. Rather, we want to become aware of—and let go of—any needy energy that we might have subconsciously hooked into.

CHAPTER 10

ARE WE BEING CALLED TO CHANGE?

Change offers us opportunities to grow, to become the person we were born to be. Change, however, is not always easy, even when we know it's going to better our lives. Why? Because it usually involves the release of an old, unresolved issue, an old way of behaving, an old way of thinking, or an old way of doing something that we've attached ourselves to. It's a letting go of things we've been attached to—and that can be painful. Change often comes in the form of pain, so our duty as spiritual seekers is to inquire constantly, "Am I being called to change?" As we know, it is natural to resist or even fear change, because we've grown attached to what is familiar. But by careful questioning, we can discover those aspects of our lives that, if changed, could bring us closer to our soul-self.

To explore this question fully, I recommend writing it down on a 3x5 card and carrying it around with you for a few days. Meditate on it. Run the question over and over in your mind: "Am I being called to change?" Or, to phrase it another way, "Is there something in my life that I should change?" If you suspect something isn't right in your career, for example, you can ask, "If there is something in my career that I am to change right now, what might that be?" Through meditation, and through the simple act of paying attention, you may begin to notice signs that had previously escaped you. Hopefully, you will come to some realization before a Mack truck runs into you with the element of change flashing in its headlights! By paying attention, after a few hours or a few days, an answer will come. Don't over-think it, when you know, you know. Trust it. The change may be small. Indeed, as I often say in my classes, incremental changes are the most successful, because they're easier to commit to and, over time, they lead to greater change. Others might notice the change, but most importantly, *you notice* that you—and your life—have changed.

You probably already have a sense of what needs to change. Maybe you have an inkling that something isn't quite right in your relationship, or in your friendships, or with your health. Answering these questions puts you touch with what you already know deep down, *that you are being called to change.* Sit with a question. The answer is already inside you, nestled in your soul. Allow yourself to sense, to hear, even to see the answer. Suddenly you will know, "This is what I'm to move towards. This is what I'm to release."

Oh, but if only that was the end of it. Once you realize what you need to change, then comes the hard slog of actually committing to the change. Imagine that we ask what it's time to change and the answer is, "The self-doubt that's been holding me back." We've always known we had some negative self-talk: we tell ourselves, "I can't do anything right," or "Things never work out for me," and we talk ourselves out of making any big changes. This old belief is limiting us. Maybe it's already ruined a perfectly good relationship, maybe it's cost us our job. After some self-examination, we've discovered we're being called to let go of that belief. Now comes the scary and possibly painful work of shedding that old belief, so that a new, confident self can emerge.

Luckily, the beautiful thing about transformational work is that once we begin to do the work, life responds in kind. As we begin to ask ourselves, "What would my life be like if I didn't limit myself with negative self-talk?" the possibility of realizing that answer increases. Imagine it—and it becomes possible.

On Fear

Even when we know it's time to change something in our lives, fear of change can hold us back. Once again, change is not easy, and one of the biggest hurdles is our unconscious resistance. If we think change is going to hurt us, we'll try to prevent it from happening. If we see change as beneficial, there's a better chance we'll find a way to surrender to it.

If we think change will hurt, we'll try to prevent it.

Fear is natural. We fear the unknown, we fear losing control, we fear death, we might even fear life itself. It's okay to experience fear, but we still have to embrace it, go through it, and learn from it. Eleanor Roosevelt said, "We must do the thing we think we cannot do." Ralph Waldo Emerson said, "Do the thing you fear, and the death of fear is certain." There is nothing wrong with feeling afraid—allowing fear to hold you back is the problem. When we confront fear and embrace it as critical for our growth, we gift ourselves with the possibility of reaching higher than we ever dreamed possible.

Let's say we're a salesperson with a great fear of talking to strangers. We spend our days puttering about the office, putting on a big show of being busy, but the busyness is just a cover for all the things we're resisting out of fear. We're not engaging with our clients; we're not making any sales. The only way out of the bind we've created is to take a deep breath, trust the process, and have one terrifying conversation with a stranger. Maybe, just maybe, that one conversation will make the next one a bit easier, and soon, we've proven that we can do that thing that paralyzed us for so long. Properly understood, the salesperson facing their fears not only accomplishes professional goals, but the salesperson attains the powerful knowledge that the only thing holding them back is their belief that they can't move forward.

So, just by becoming aware, by paying attention to what's really going on, we can give ourselves permission to show up in a different way. We can acknowledge our fears. We can acknowledge that facing our fears is by definition scary—and we can do it anyway.

As noted earlier, Erica Jong put it this way: "I have accepted...the fear of change. I have gone ahead despite the pounding in my heart that says: turn back." There's a golden nugget of truth in those words. Yes, your heart may pound. Yes, your knees may tremble. But you know that what you deeply desire lies on the other side of your fear. This is the key: accept fear and fear dissolves.

Problems are Meant to be Guidelines, Not Stop Signs

Problems are on purpose. Problems are there for a reason. Life doesn't stop because we've got a problem to solve: rather, the work of our life lies in confronting our problems. Problems help us to heal and grow. Correctly identifying what the problem is and then embracing that problem unlocks the transformative process.

Most people run away from their problems, not realizing that problems are like the emergency lighting in the aisle of an airplane, guiding them to a way out. As Robert Schuller stated in one of his sermons, *problems are guidelines, not stop signs.* Avoiding a problem creates stress; stress creates resistance; resistance creates unnecessary pain. Instead of running from a problem, we must learn to recognize the problem as a message revealing an issue we're meant to be working through. If we're running away from the problem, we're also running away from the solution.

Some people believe that if they acquire enough money or enough love, all of their problems will go away. That's simply not true. Ask anyone who has suddenly come into a large amount of money or who finds themselves surrounded by a plethora of companions. They'll tell you that a sudden change in fortune doesn't solve any of life's underlying problems; in most cases, it just adds another level of complexity. Problems get resolved by recognizing the reason the problem is there in the first place. Surrendering gives us the space to tackle problems head-on.

We must be willing and ready to let go of that which is no longer working in our lives. Remember, the pain and problems of life can be our teachers. Once we've had enough troubles, we'll honor the call to change. At some point in our trials and tribulations, we come to a tipping point. We have to let go of our need to resist *what is*—those inner feelings and outer experiences are letting us know—it's time to change.

So, ask yourself, "Does this relationship truly serve me and my life? Does this activity, or way of behaving still serve me? Is there something in my life right now that's no longer working for me?"

As we release our resistance to letting go of things that no longer serve us, we open the doorway to new changes. To embrace the new, we must create space for it to enter our lives by letting go of the old. When we accept our problem, the solution comes—because we have created space for it.

As we fully accept what is, the resistance we felt simply falls away and we feel serene. One of the signs of true acceptance is a feeling of *serenity*. This prayer, used in Twelve-Step groups, can be helpful when working on letting go of resistance:

> *God, grant me the serenity*
> *to accept the things I cannot change;*
> *courage to change the things I can;*
> *and wisdom to know the difference."*

-adapted from "The Serenity Prayer" by Reinhold Niebuhr

Change and the Status Quo

The status quo is comfortable. When we are living in the status quo, things aren't that bad, but we're not growing at all. You'll see this with entrepreneurs who have built a successful small business but allow it to languish, to stagnate even, because it's easier to be moderately successful than to risk it all in pursuit of grander success. You'll see it in relationships too, where both partners are moderately satisfied—nothing is terribly wrong—but still, it's not great. In some cases, the status quo is perfectly okay; there's no need to mess with a good situation just for the sake of change. But sometimes a mediocre status quo is that first whisper of the call to change, the proverbial feather alighting upon our path, letting us know it's time to move.

We can consider the status quo as a kind of autopilot. Is some aspect of our life on autopilot? Is there some aspect of our life that we've been neglecting, allowing it to stagnate in the status quo? What is it? Is it the first, quiet call to change? In other words, is there some part of our life that we've been holding onto out of habit? Might that something snowball into something larger, a more intractable problem, if we don't address it now? Again, some things are worth holding onto, sometimes the status quo is a sign that things are exactly as they should be. But at other times, the status quo is the result of us hanging onto something we should be letting go of.

Letting go of the old is crucial for embracing the new.

As we learn to identify those situations in which the status quo is a call to change, we can prevent ourselves from entering the painful loop of ego-driven resistance and unhealthy coping mechanisms. It can be hard to let go, but letting go of the old is crucial for embracing the new. Freedom comes when we let go completely.

As noted earlier, think of the last relationship you had. How did it end? How soon did you become aware that it was time to let go? Were you loving and respectful? Answering these questions gives you an opportunity to check where you're at in developing your natural ability to let go of things that no longer serve you.

So, are you ready and willing to let go? Remember, the pain of letting go is teaching you lessons you need to learn. I find that most people hold onto the old, taking on more and more pain, until they hit their threshold. For some people, the pain threshold is the discomfort of the status quo, others suffer the pain of resistance until they can't hang on for one more minute. We all reach our tipping point. To avoid the unnecessary pain along the way, we have to identify the call to change early on. Once we do, there's no turning back. We're moving towards the change we've been seeking—and that change has also been seeking us. Welcome it!

 **Exercises**

For the exercises below, take some quiet time by yourself. Get still. Picture your higher self.

If you don't have an image of your higher self or your soul just yet, picture the words "Higher Self" on the screen of your mind. Place these words right over your heart. With your journal and pen in hand, read these questions. Go with the first answer that comes to you—write it down. Over time, the answers to these questions will change as you change. Be authentic. Stay in the moment—and breathe!

1) Is there something I am to change in my life (personally or professionally)? What is it?

2) Is there something I am afraid of changing in my life right now? What is it? What about that thing am I afraid of?

3) What might happen to me—or in my life—if I were to change this?

4) If I make this change, how might I change? How might my life change?

5) When was the last time I made a change? What change did I make? Did I celebrate the change? If so, what did I do to celebrate?

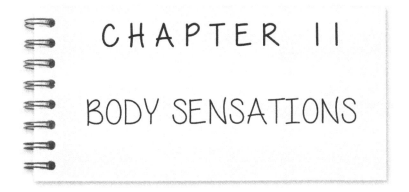

CHAPTER 11

BODY SENSATIONS

If we haven't healed our relationship with our feelings, if we haven't embraced the call to change, odds are that our unconscious resistance can take center stage—and can begin to show up in the physical body. The body is your best tool for transformational work, and as you begin to pay attention to the subtle (and not-so-subtle) dynamics at play in your body, you discover that there is a wealth of information available about where your resistance lies. As mentioned earlier, there are three key locations in the body where resistance will show itself: the throat, the center of the chest, and the solar plexus.

Unconscious Resistance in the Body

The moment we become activated, our unconscious resistance manifests in one or more of those three areas. This is where the energy becomes tight or tense. One way to check this is when things haven't been going your way. You've been trying to make something happen that's clearly not happening. Stop what you're doing and place your attention on these three areas, one at a time, to see if one or more are tight or tense. If they are, that's unconscious resistance that you're now becoming aware of. This is your body's way of letting you know that you're in resistance about someone or something in your life. I'll share more on how to clear the resistance in the body later in one of the twelve suggested Transformational Practices. But for now, it is enough to know that when you are resisting change psychically, your body reflects it. You feel tense and inflexible, because in effect, you are. The body doesn't lie: if you feel pain in your body, you can take that to mean that there's some psychological pain under the surface. Your body is speaking to you, demanding that you address the source of your suffering.

The body has its own intelligence—which the chiropractic profession refers to as "innate intelligence." Other healing modalities call it "body wisdom." Your body can become your best tool for transformation; this is why it's so important to take good care of your body. The body is a temple for the soul but most people spend more time and energy taking care of their homes or their automobiles! When we start taking care of our bodies, our life experience improves.

The language of the body is *sensation*. If you've numbed out your natural ability to feel, you've temporarily shut down your capacity to hear your body speaking to you. As a result, your body might help you to transform by manifesting a painful situation or physical condition. (It would be easier to re-establish your connection with your body so you can receive its communication without manifesting a painful condition or illness!) Pain in the body can often be an invitation to heal something about you and your life.

Pain can be an invitation to heal something in your life.

The key here is to learn how to dialogue with bodily sensations. It's like opening up a conversation—we begin by noticing what we sense, what we experience in the body, without shutting it down. It's so important to repair our relationship with our feelings because if we resist them, if we attempt to push the pain away, then we don't connect with the body and we could miss the body's signals as it tries to let us know we need to let go of something.

I remember a time many years ago when I first became aware of my body communicating with me. I had been doing a relatively deep cleanse and one night, suddenly I could actually see my liver as if I was in a movie theater watching it on a screen. My liver began to speak to me. I know this might sound crazy, but it was the first time I realized that I had many feelings buried within me, and, more specifically, that my liver carried unresolved anger from my past. At the time, I didn't know it, but energetically (or emotionally, or subconsciously) speaking, the liver is the anger center of the body.

As noted, the body's organs communicate through sensation—or, one might say *telepathically*. Suddenly, we become aware of something, it is as if we hear with our inner hearing. I had heard my liver! At the time, I had no idea *why* I had the unresolved anger, I had not yet unlocked or released those past memories. But, shortly after this experience, the past events attached to this unresolved anger began to surface.

When I was younger, I dealt with my emotions by stuffing them, repressing them as fast as I could. Back in those days, I was incredibly addicted to food—more specifically, to the chemicals in junk food. I ate a lot of processed foods and overdid it to the point that I caused myself physical problems. I used food as a way to suppress the emotions that I simply did not want to or know *how to* deal with then. That experience changed everything for me. Since then, I have found it extremely beneficial to open up to receiving what my body is saying to me—and then I decide to do whatever is in my best interest. In doing this, I am supporting my physical body—and it is supporting me.

Getting in touch with the intelligence of our bodies, really listening, and then acting on the messages we receive is another way of realigning with our higher selves and with our soul-selves.

Learn to Relax

To get good at embracing change in our lives, we must learn how to relax our bodies, minds, and spirits. We must slow down and perhaps even calm down. The best things are found when we're moving slowly in life, both outwardly and inwardly. This way, we notice everything. We catch everything. We pick up on nuances. We become more intuitive as slowing down allows us to listen within.

Regular daily meditation can help you to slow down the pace of life. Meditation is a learned skill, anyone can learn how to do it. If you're not good at meditating or slowing things down just yet, start with just ten to fifteen minutes each day. That might look like going to the park and sitting on bench, studying the birds, or focusing on a tree. Keep it simple. Decide on something that you'll concentrate on for the next thirty consecutive days—this will help train your mind to listen and help you relax into your body. If you are stressed during the process of change, your meditation time is a time to be easier on yourself.

In the process of letting go to embrace change, many people get really stressed. Does it have to be that way? Of course not. But in many cases, that's how it is until we decide we're going to show up differently. And, one of the ways to show up differently is to cut ourselves some slack. In fact, you might even take time on purpose. Take a break from whatever is stressing you, even if it's just for a few minutes. Put your mind on something else. Stressing will only make the experience of change more intense. Taking a nap, going for a walk, or meditating for fifteen or twenty minutes can make a huge difference. Then, you can look at what was stressing you with fresh eyes.

Take Care of Your Body

I had some friends who were incredible transformational teachers and healers. They were beautiful people doing great work in the community. The community loved them and they loved creating a transformational space. Unfortunately, they didn't do this type of cleansing or releasing, they didn't take care of their own bodies because it meant having to confront their addictions to food and alcohol. As a result, they both passed in their forties. It was sad because they were loved and appreciated by so many people for the service they provided. Even though they were encouraged to cleanse and release, they didn't, and eventually, their lifestyle caught up with them.

I've seen this scenario play out in many people's lives. They end up with unnecessary problems, problems that could have been prevented if only they had learned to take care of their bodies, to adopt a daily cleansing program, and to operate from a level of higher awareness about the importance of maintaining peak health through cleansing.

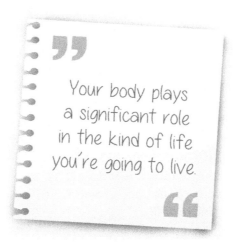

Your body plays a significant role in the kind of life you're going to live.

Remember, your body plays a significant role in the kind of life you're going to live, and you need your body to live that life! So, one of the most important principles in living your best life is *to become better at taking care of your body*. As mentioned before, your body can become your best tool for transformation. It can give you the energy you need to embrace the changes that come knocking on your door. The energy for transformation comes through from the body and you can use it to embrace what you're changing in your world.

So, to keep the body's energy at an optimum level, practice good self-care, inside and out, every day. Maybe you'll sit in silence every day. Maybe you'll stretch, journal, get acupuncture, take power naps, get to bed earlier at night, get good quality colon therapy, or choose to give your body a rest by taking vacation time. Maybe you'll attend seminars that you are drawn to, or find a transformational teacher, life coach, or therapist that is truly right for you. Or, maybe you'll take rest from eating or do a one-to-three-day water or juice fast. Whatever taking care of your body looks like for you, it will pay off as your body returns to optimum health and you have all the energy you need to transform your life.

Self-Care, Inside and Out

As beneficial as all the previously mentioned forms of self-care will be for us, it's also ultra-important to exercise—and to discover the *right kind of exercise* for our own physical capacities. As a young man, this is where I began creating problems for myself that at that time I wasn't even aware of. You see, I thought that if I just focused on improving my physical strength, everything would be fine. But I never created a strong foundation for my physical wellbeing later in life, just as I see so many young people doing today. The deeper purpose of exercise is to get stagnant energy moving. When the energy is moving, the body does better. For example, if you exercise too much or exceed your capabilities, you'll be sore or exhausted for a few days. That doesn't help the energy move. Instead, it creates resistance as you try to protect yourself from feeling sore and/or exhausted.

When it comes to taking good care of our bodies, we need not only to exercise regularly and nourish ourselves, but we need also to be mindful that everything we take into the body is to our highest benefit. For example, there are numerous substances that are part of modern society's wellness system that we are told are good for us…but in fact, our body cannot fully absorb or release them on its own. Synthetic ingredients of any kind, for example, can be toxic to our bodies. Medicines such as antibiotics too, can prove to be more detrimental than beneficial, if not taken with full awareness and in moderation. I saw this with myself in the first thirty years of my life when I lived on different kinds of medication, especially antibiotics. I watched this play out with my Dad in his last couple of years, which were extremely painful for him. For example, even though on some level it looked like his medications were saving his life, for years leading up to his death, he complained of painful constipation—and he wasn't interested in alternative health options. Throughout Dad's life, he never really let go of anything, he lived his life in a state of 'hanging on.' This is when I first noticed the connection between the health of the colon and the way we live our lives.

You see, the key function of the colon is to eliminate, to let go of that which is no longer serving the body. For example, if you have a pattern of holding on to things—people, projects, and/or situations in your life—that you really should let go of, over time this can manifest in your body as constipation, which can be very painful. Colonics and enemas have become popular as they can help the colon to release, rather than getting jammed up with old waste and toxins.

If constipation is an issue for us, it is beneficial to explore where we're at with our choices around letting go of things that are no longer working. We could acknowledge that we have a problem with letting go in our life, period. Then we can ask, "Why? Why am I so committed to hanging onto this old way of doing things? What am I afraid of? What need might be influencing the choice to keep me hanging on?" Whatever the answers are, can we give ourselves permission right now to let go of that needy energy? What's driving our choice to hang on? There's a purpose or a reason behind everything, and the way to get to it is through asking the right questions—and then answering them honestly and taking positive action.

Internal Cleansing

Just as we regularly clean the insides of our homes, offices, and automobiles, cleaning the insides of our bodies ought to be a regular activity. Imagine not cleaning the inside of your house for months or even years! How would this impact your life? Choosing to cleanse your body internally once or twice a year can be beneficial, as Millan Chessman writes in her book, *Cleanse Internally*. Realize that your health is your wealth—it affects you and your loved ones. The question becomes: *How do you see your health on a scale of 1 to 10?* What level of importance do you give your health? Do you have a health-promoting lifestyle? Or have you been taking your health for granted? Your body ought to become your best ally, for without a vibrant and healthy body, you limit your ability to transform your life.

So, what's the best internal cleanse to use? It's always best to consult with a holistic healthcare practitioner to determine this. Even if you've been feeling intuitively that it's time to do an internal cleanse on your own, your holistic practitioner can help you decide, for example, if a sea salt water flush might be beneficial or if you should include colon hydrotherapy, a series of colonics administered over a period of time. Whatever you choose, research your options, speak to your wellness consultant and a colon hydrotherapist, and let them help you determine what is best for you and your body.

There are many success stories proving how effective colon hydrotherapy can be. In one such story, for example, a man named Marc Herlands owes his life to colonics. Herlands and his physician, M.D. Gary Shima, wrote the book: *The Art of Healing*, wherein they tell the remarkable story of Marc healing his body. When Marc first saw Dr. Shima, his symptoms were deep depression, suicidal ideation, exhaustive chronic fatigue, chronic muscle pain, morbid obesity, swollen lymph glands in his neck, and a major sleep disorder. When treatment stopped working shortly after it began, Dr. Shima was convinced that a significant portion of Marc's problem stemmed from his body's accumulation of heavy metals. So, he ordered Marc to use colon hydrotherapy. Marc felt better after the first treatment. And that was just the beginning—over the next few years, he released almost all the toxins and heavy metals that had accumulated in his lifetime. To quote Marc, "As the level of toxins in my body lessened, I slowly regained my health. Colonics indeed saved my life."

It's helpful to educate yourself on colon hydrotherapy before starting a course of treatment. There are some really good books written on this subject, and as Chessman strongly recommends in *Cleanse Internally*, "Clients must be careful that their colon hydrotherapists are fully qualified, certified and recommended by others." A good hydrotherapist can be a godsend, especially when we're doing a deep physical cleanse. It helps to keep everything moving—and a clean colon is a happy colon.

The Lymph System

To have a happy colon, you've got to know a little bit about the significance of your lymph system. Someone explained the lymphatic system to me years ago: it's like the indoor plumbing in your house. When it comes to deep cleansing, it's wise to include the lymph system as it's the garbage dump in the body for toxic waste. Colonics help not just the colon, they promote the expulsion of toxic material from the lymph system. There are a few ways we can stimulate the lymph system to eliminate toxic waste: jumping up and down on a trampoline, jumping up and down without a trampoline, a lymph massage by a massage therapist, and vigorous walking or marching. Movement is key for good lymph and colon health.

When we are aware of how the lymph system and the colon function, we become dedicated to treating these parts of our bodies in the healthiest way possible. On a regular basis, we want to release the toxins and waste that are no longer serving our bodies.

To gain optimum health and the stamina to live life to the fullest, we need to make releasing toxins and eliminating waste a constant thing, a regular part of our healthy lifestyle.

Detoxing as Transformation

Whether toxicity is physical, mental, emotional, or spiritual, it's important to detox annually or biannually—and to do so strategically. We have to consciously choose to let go of toxic substances, toxic thoughts, and toxic emotions that we've picked up through simply living our lives. Dr. Joseph Pizzorno, the founder of Bastyr University (the country's first and largest fully accredited university of natural medicine) and author of the book, *The Toxic Solution*, states, "While lifestyle, diet, and genetics all play a major role in your health, symptoms of declining health and chronic disease often start with toxic overload." He is convinced that lifelong good health rests on two key determinants: your exposure to toxins and your body's ability to process them.

Detoxing as a way of life is another key to truly embracing change in our world—we're detoxing all the stuff that's no longer working, no longer serving. If our bodies are backed up with high levels of toxicity, at the very least, it's going to prevent the body from performing at optimal levels. Letting go of toxicity can open us up to experiencing and actualizing greater possibilities—and in some cases, can even save us from a path of ruin! Learning how to release toxins is clearly key in mastering the art of change.

If you are doing a complete internal cleansing program with colonics, remember to use a good probiotic to help replace the good bacteria in your body. Colonics not only clear out negative bacteria, they also clear positive bacteria, so including a probiotic in your cleansing program is good practice.

Our Online Community

Visit my website at *www.DaleHalaway.com* as I'll be posting videos and recordings of talks and radio shows on a variety of topics, including my transformational healing program. There will also be links to my tele-class series, live seminars, online courses and books, and a collection of research links that can help you as you move forward on your healing and transformational journey. You're invited to join our global online community of seekers—I look forward to connecting with you!

 **Exercises**

For the exercises below, take some quiet time by yourself. Get still. Picture your higher self.

If you don't have an image of your higher self or your soul just yet, picture the words "Higher Self" on the screen of your mind. Place these words right over your heart. With your journal and pen in hand, read these questions. Go with the first answer that comes to you—write it down. Over time, the answers to these questions will change as you change. Be authentic. Stay in the moment—and breathe!

1) What could you do right now to minimize or release stress? Could you take a walk, go and meditate, or do some processing or journaling?

2) In practicing good self-care, what could you do for yourself today, or even this week?

3) What is your favorite way to exercise? Riding your bicycle, going to the gym, swimming, doing yoga, dancing, etc.? When is your best time of day to exercise?

4) On a scale of 1 to 10 (1 being very little, 10 being a lot), how well do you listen to your body? Write that number in your journal. When was the last time you listened to your body? Did it pay off?

5) When was the last time you did a cleanse? How did you feel after the cleanse? Would it be beneficial for you to do a cleanse or detox soon? How much do you know about detoxing or cleansing? Do you have a health care practitioner with whom you could discuss doing a cleanse?

CHAPTER 12

WORKING WITH CHANGE

What can help us to transform? The answer: energy. Yes, energy. It takes energy to change. Stress takes energy. Love releases energy. When we're in love with what we're doing and the person we're in a relationship with, for example, we get energy naturally. If we're not enjoying what we're doing or the person we're with, it takes energy and increases our stress. If we take care of the body, it gives us energy. If we abuse the body, it takes energy and at some point, we'll feel depleted. Dr. Donald Epstein, the founder of EPI-Energetics™ and Wise World Seminars, states that "Progress requires change and change requires energy." Dr. Epstein goes on to say, "With most people, the highest vision they hold within themselves is to survive, which is when they are energy-poor. Whereas someone who is energy-rich has a higher vision to thrive."

So, we understand that transformation and change require energy, and we know that the more we take care of our energy, the better we take care of ourselves. More specifically, the more energy we have, the more it can support us, in going the distance, and in truly embracing the changes that come knocking on our doors. Without the energy to transform ourselves, we'll simply find ourselves just getting by in our relationships, in our businesses, and/or in our careers while maintaining the status quo.

There are a number of beneficial transformational systems in the marketplace today—the key, of course, is finding the one that works best for you, to replenish and rejuvenate your energy. Here are a few methods worthy of mention: EMDR, which stands for Eye Movement Desensitization and Reprocessing Therapy; EFT, Emotional Freedom Technique; Family or Systemic Constellation work; and the TransCovery Process®.

EMDR can be used for a range of emotional issues, including PTSD, anxiety, clearing emotional trauma, and a whole lot more.

EFT is a psychological acupressure technique that I use in my seminars. EFT is easy to learn. Through simple fingertip tapping, you input kinetic energy to specific meridians on the head and chest. EFT tapping removes negative emotions as you think about problems, points of pain, traumatic events, or do positive affirmations. I recommend this method to anyone wishing to improve their emotional health.

Another effective tool for powerful change is Family Constellation work, also known as Systemic Constellation work. A Family Constellation is a method that allows you to discover the invisible dynamics that underlie your current emotional and energetic challenges. These dynamics often involve your original family, your present family, and/or your ancestral past. This transformative modality, developed by psychotherapist Bert Hellinger, among others, reveals to us the ways in which we subconsciously carry the unresolved issues of previous generations. Family Constellation work brings unresolved issues into conscious awareness, allowing you to resolve them and let them go.

Finally, my TransCovery Process® helps unlock emotional energy that's been hindering us in moving forward. I based this simple system on self-inquiry—raising our conscious awareness of the needy self by calling it up from the subconscious to the conscious level on a regular basis. (Remember the garden analogy mentioned earlier? TransCovery™ is like plucking weeds daily, keeping the inner garden clear of unwanted growth that can zap the nutrition we need to thrive.)

As noted earlier, the needy self constantly resists someone or something in our lives. This is the number one way the ego can—and will, if we're not mindful—prevent us from moving forward in our lives.

By clearing needy energy on a regular basis, we simultaneously unlock old, emotional energy that's trapped within the subconscious and/or in the physical body. TransCovery™ not only helps us to clear this suppressed energy, it also re-centers and stabilizes us within a matter of minutes.

The ego can – and will, if we're not mindful – prevent us from moving forward in our lives.

Is EMDR, EFT, Family Constellation Work, The TransCovery Process®, or another transformational system you're working with right for you? Check with your gut, run it up your own inner flagpole if you will. If the answer is yes, get started on the program you choose, check it out—and see how it goes. Once you start getting results, you can proceed further, using what you have learned through your chosen modality to help you embrace change and revitalize your energy, so you can step fully into your own transformational experience.

The Transformational Power of Momentum

When it comes to transformation, we want to move forward powerfully, with momentum. Just as with anything we are building—creating a loving, healthy relationship, advancing our career or business—somewhere along our journey, we notice that something feels vastly different. It's like we're lifted higher, we're energized, we're supported in a way we have not been before. This is called *momentum* and this extra energy makes us feel engaged; we experience more fun, more ease, and are genuinely more interested in and fascinated with life.

If you've been resisting change instead of embracing change…if life is not moving forward easily, it's because you haven't yet truly committed. Once you decide you are genuinely intent on transforming yourself, once you are working towards your goals, and you choose the right program for you, *you will experience momentum*. As that momentum rises, it picks you up, elevates your experience, and propels you forward into positive change. So, are you ready? It's time to transform!

Find a Transformational Teacher

Finding the right transformational teacher is essential for the seeker who wants to experience true transformation. I first recognized the significance of a good teacher back in the days of building sales organizations: those salespersons who had the right coach, therapist, and/or mentor to assist them by far outperformed those who didn't. They were highly successful: they had *momentum*. As noted, experiencing momentum requires using the right program, and good programs are directed by qualified mentors, trained to bring us back to our inner selves, where all the meaningful truths and most profound discoveries are made. Our coach will meet us where we're at and take us further, acting as a role model, offering sage-like advice, helping to raise our awareness. Mentors inspire us to connect with ourselves, to take the right kind of action, and to embrace change. Without the right teachers in our lives, it will take much longer to get where we're going.

Many times, those who don't rise as high as they could eschew mentorship, saying, essentially, "I don't need this. I already know this," or, "I can do all of this by myself." I've often said, "If that's true, why didn't God give you your own island?" And of course, when we're acting this way, the universe responds accordingly: "Alright, do it all by yourself, you know it all." Usually, that person struggles twice as much as the individual who has the right teacher, the right coach, or the right mentor. The person who has opted for help *knows* the value of having a teacher in their lives—personally and/or professionally. The truth is, we all do much better and we can travel much faster on our journey with help.

Our job, first and foremost, ought to be to ensure we are rising to the challenge of being a good student. Being a good student is so important, all of the great teachers were, at one point, great students. In fact, they still might be great students because they've embodied learning as part of their lifestyle. Great teachers, whether mentoring others in relationships, success, business, health, finances, spirituality, transformation, or the martial arts, bring their students to the doorway of experiences that cause change and growth, and then they step aside. They don't do the work, that would keep students dependent. Rather, they teach students how to prepare for the next life-enriching, life-altering event. They let their students experience whatever comes. If a teacher is with you for some time, they'll be on the other side of the doorway you just walked through, waiting to celebrate your success.

Another way to find support in your transformational process is to find a buddy. By being willing to work with a buddy, you can engage with someone who is travelling along a similar path. They too are embracing change and so can provide support that you can benefit from, just as they can benefit from your support. Now, to clarify, this support person is not a mentor, coach, or therapist—they are just a buddy. Even though your teacher, therapist, and mentor also support you, there's a distinction: your buddy is there whenever you need him or her, to talk with, to share with, and to understand in a deep way what your transformational journey looks and feels like.

Love and Acceptance

What is your capacity for love and acceptance in your day-to-day life? Can you embrace all your feelings just as they are? If you feel anger or jealousy, can you allow yourself to acknowledge it, to just own it—without acting out or projecting it onto someone else? Can you just be angry or jealous? What we can't own, we can't change.

Love and acceptance *of what is* is the soul-self in action, it's the divine in us, just being. When we bring complete love and acceptance to whatever it is we're dealing with, that energy changes, it transforms—it *shifts*. That is the power of love and acceptance, they stimulate movement. We can choose at any time to love and accept someone or something, regardless of who they are or what that is. With the complete acceptance of *what is* comes tremendous freedom.

The act of loving and accepting naturally calls our soul forth, allowing our spiritual energy to flow out and empower us, elevating us to the higher vibration of the soul-self, beyond the lower vibration ego-self.

One of the tricks of the ego-self is to shift us from love and acceptance into fear and judgement. By judging, we make whatever we're dealing with wrong, we lock what is wrong into place. And, by locking it into place, we become stuck. This is a trick of the ego, because when the ego gets us stuck, it stays safe. Remember, the ego is afraid of moving forward. Once we make someone or something wrong, energy stops moving. Of course, all judgement can be traced to self-judgement—another ego trick—it loves to create complexity. Judgement is a way of resisting, another way the ego protects itself. If the ego can get us to stay in resistance by judging someone or something, its influence over us is strengthened. The ego doesn't care if that means repeating the same old issue or painful experience over and over again.

In my life, there was always someone or something that I found myself resisting because I didn't feel safe, even though most times I really was safe. There was always something for me to hold in judgement, and then I would become afraid of that very thing. This is how I stayed in resistance. Of course, I was unconscious about this back then, it would have been more painful had I been conscious! But along the way, my life let me know that something wasn't working; I frequently found myself in similar upsetting experiences. But each time there were different "cast members," among them, my Dad. The pain of this constant drama was unbearable at times. I came across a quote credited to Ralph Waldo Emerson and I would say it out loud over and over again: "What lies behind us and what lies before us are tiny matters compared to what lies within us."

One day, something happened that inspired me and I decided to learn to love and accept my Dad just as he was. So, I did. That was the starting point of the many changes I've experienced in my life since then. To love and accept what is, in our day-to-day lives, is incredibly freeing. Our minds settle down and maybe even go quiet from time to time. Imagine having a quiet, completely peaceful mind! What would that be like? Imagine your body calming down, beginning to feel more relaxed, feeling more comfortable in your own skin.

My hope is that checking in with yourself about *where you are at currently in your natural ability to love and accept what's going on in your world* might illuminate your path and help to facilitate change. Whether what arises when you ask this question is something to do with your physical body, your finances, your relationships, or whatever, checking in can be truly illuminating. Discovering the truth can be the catalyst for change.

Another way of accessing the truth within you is to ask yourself if you sit in judgement of anyone (and that 'anyone' could be *you*), or anything—and if you do, what are you judging? We can get stuck in the maze of our own judgements for weeks, months, even years. The way out is learning to love and accept ourselves just as we are. It is liberating for us when we come into complete acceptance of ourselves, quirks and all. So, can you accept what is, right now? Can you love and accept yourself just as you are? Whatever arises, as you get better at loving and accepting things the way they are, stuck energy moves, judgement falls away, a new awareness arises within you, and everything begins to change for the better.

 **Exercises**

For the exercises below, take some quiet time by yourself. Get still. Picture your higher self.

If you don't have an image of your higher self or your soul just yet, picture the words "Higher Self" on the screen of your mind. Place these words right over your heart. With your journal and pen in hand, read these questions. Go with the first answer that comes to you—write it down. Over time, the answers to these questions will change as you change. Be authentic. Stay in the moment—and breathe!

1) Is there someone in your life you could be more loving and accepting of? Who? What about them could you be more loving and accepting of?

2) Could you give yourself permission to be loving and accepting of this person right now?

3) Is there some part of you that you could be more loving and accepting of right now? What part? What about this part of you could you be more loving and accepting of?

4) Could you give yourself permission to be loving and accepting of this part of you right now?

The Triad for Transformation

As noted, the Triad for Transformation is made up of three pillars of awareness which comprise the foundation of all successful transformation. Each pillar is named for the attribute it represents—and each name begins with the letter S. When you remain mindful of what each pillar symbolizes, committed to developing that pillar to its fullest potential, and steadfast in your quest to become your best self, you lay the groundwork for realizing positive change.

Let's imagine the triad as a *triangle*. The triangle has three significant points (or vertices) which, when joined together create a robust structure that can withstand pretty much anything. If one of those vertices is broken or disconnected, however, a little pressure applied to the triangle is enough to collapse it.

The first pillar of the triad, in the apex of our triangle, is *spirit* as in "soul." The second is *structure* as in "support," and the third is *strategy* as in "system."

Spirit

As noted, the first S pillar in the Triad is for "spirit" or soul, our spiritual-self or the spiritual essence of life. If you know in your heart of hearts that you are ready to do your soul work, if you are ready to transform and move from an egoic place to a soulful place, a helpful spiritual exercise is to ask yourself, "What are my values when it comes to transformation and my own personal growth? Where am I at with my personal life? Where do I need to go and what do I need to do to empower myself? What are my deepest or truest core values? What are the values of my loved ones? What are the values of the key team members in my organization? Do these people share my values? Are their values unified with mine?"

Asking these questions brings depth to the work you are doing on a transformational level. The answers must come not only from the mind and heart but also from the soul. When you ask and answer these questions, your transformation becomes richer, more expansive, broader, more complete, as you infuse your everyday life with the essence of your soul.

In everything you do, you must ask yourself, "Is this activity in alignment with my soul? Or is this action being motivated by my ego?" Being mindful and vigilant about who is in control—ego or soul—is key. When you do this on a regular basis, you begin to understand the marked difference between being under the influence of your ego persona, and being aligned with your soul. When your life is in alignment with your soul, you live differently, you experience things in a new way. For example, you only have close friendships that support you and empower you, people who help you to maintain your inner balance. You start to let go of people and things that don't inspire you or uplift you.

This kind of transformation doesn't happen overnight—at least not usually! The ego can hang onto its habits and behaviors and it can be challenging to stay on track with embodying the soul's purpose in our day-to-day routines. Also, not everyone is ready for the next level. If your life is not in alignment with your soul yet, it is going to be almost impossible to really honor the voice of your soul, to allow your soul to come into your body, to take over your mind, to vanquish your ego, and to liberate your true essence from the bondage of the ego.

The essence of who we really are is always reflected in our relationship with someone or something—such as our family, community, business, or organization. It's in the relationships we create in interactive units that our deepest values are expressed. I've often said that our core values are changeless because they're encoded in the DNA of our soul-self, our true essence. In our early years, many of us create values based on what someone else thinks—but those values are not *our* values. However, if we're not aware of that, we live our life based on someone else's values. And while that's all going on, our core values are buried, inert. When an individual realizes they're living someone else's values, they can uncover and reactivate their own values through the transformational process. Through self-development and self-discovery, they find their way to this first S of the Triad, the *soul-self*. Thereafter, everything in life becomes meaningful and fulfilling as they live life anew, expressing themselves freely and openly from their own value system. Following are three ways to access our core values, our true essence.

1. First, we can *focus on who we want to become*. To do this, we choose someone we respect, admire, and look up to, to serve as a positive, healthy role model. Perhaps we want to be like that person—not *be* that person, but *be like* that person, emulating their characteristics and values. But the truth is that we already are the person we want to become—our true identity is buried deep within us and when we're transforming, we're peeling away these layers. As we get deeper, we uncover our true self. As we watch our role model demonstrate their highest and best qualities, they inspire us to engage with similar values encoded within our core-self. We touch, see, and connect with our own core value system—and begin the process of embodying and demonstrating our true essence.

2. The second way to access our essence is to question ourselves any time it comes time to make a change: "Where is the influence or incentive to change coming from? The soul or the ego?" If it's coming from the ego, it will come through our needy self because we're attempting to make a change so that the need

hooked into that change gets met. If that's what's happening, the change will never happen.

On the other hand, if a call to change is coming from the soul, the right support and strategy will come quickly into our reality, and the appearance of this support and strategy will validate that the call is indeed coming from a soul-source. Next thing you know, we will have the right system, structure, and people in place in order to evolve to the next level. For example, the "right people" could be a like-minded group, or just one person—a tremendous coach, a mentor, a teacher, a business partner, a mate, or a friend.

In my seminars with couples and partners, at the end of the class, one member of a partnership may say, "I came here for my partner and now, going forward, I will come for myself." Something has obviously happened, they are choosing from their soul. In the beginning, they came because their partner asked them umpteen times and perhaps applied pressure as well. These participants sit with their arms folded, legs crossed, for the first thirty or forty-five minutes of Day One. Soon, however, they drop their arms, plant both feet on the floor, and sit on the end of their chairs—they become engaged and realize that this is not for their partner—it's for them. They connect to their truth—even though it might look like their partner got them to come, really their soul was merged with the soul of their partner. This is what it looks like when the impetus to change comes from the soul, not the ego.

3. The third way we can access our essence is by bringing consciousness into our day-to-day awareness. I sometimes refer to this as "soul-infusion." Soul infusion changes the way we see things—things in and of themselves haven't changed, but we see them differently. We experience an inner perceptual shift.

All true, lasting change happens first from within. This is the transformative power of inner perception. Our outer life is a manifestation of how we see it—from the inside out. This is why two people can be looking at the exact same situation or circumstance yet see it differently. You see, once our perception of something changes, everything that correlates on the outside also changes. Change the inner perception and you'll change the outer experience. Period. This is what the late Dr. Wayne Dyer meant when he said (echoing the late Max Planck), "When we change the way we look at things, the things we look at change." This ought to be our focus when it comes to being engaged in our transformational work. As we continue to do our inner work and change ourselves, we change our perception—then, it is just a matter of time until our world changes. To know and trust in that is a wise practice.

As you will see, engaging with these three methods and putting them into practice in our lives is a game changer on all levels. Often, we think we are in touch with our core values, but what's really happening is that the ego is tricking us into thinking we're living through our core values to ensure that everything stays the same. As a result, we don't make the best decisions, the right decisions, the first time around. Accessing our core values takes time and a lot of work—we have to dig deep—but when we do, we begin to live our lives authentically.

Now that we have the awareness and the intention to really bring soul into our lives (or to bring our lives into alignment with our souls), what can pull us back into the ego? How can we learn to truly infuse our lives, our businesses and/or our careers with soul? One of the key ways we can do this is by increasing our awareness so we can clearly recognize when we are living 'egoically.' We will take a deeper dive into this in book two, *Transform Your Destiny*.

When you start doing this work, you will go through a period when you catch yourself living inauthentically. There might be a sense of shallowness to it, perhaps you'll recognize, for example, that in a conversation you just had with someone, you were not truthful. You might not go back to that person and tell them you were not truthful, but you've caught yourself. You start to realize that there is something much bigger going on for you—that living your life genuinely is the path to transformation. And, once you get a taste of living life authentically, you want more of it. This fuels and inspires you to transform your life, to recognize and embrace the changes that will make your higher self—your spiritual self—active in your life.

Structure

As noted, the second S is "*structure*" and/or support. We need structure to thrive, to achieve what we want to accomplish. A great example of this would be moving our home or office: we would experience the process of moving differently if we were to do it all on our own versus having the right people in place to support us in making the move. When all the right people are in place, it makes our process flow. Similarly, when embracing change, it'll be much easier to do when the right person or the right program supports us in successfully embracing change.

Without good structure, there will always be chaos in the change process. Just as a building needs a structure to stand on, so too, we need a foundation, we need support. We can find this structure and support by building strong relationships. In our company, for example, do we have the right support team in place? In our significant relationships, are we getting the right level of support from our partner, from our friends? In our personal transformation work, is there a structure in place? Are we getting the right support from the right coach or the right teacher?

Once we get the best structures in place, amazing things can happen. As we go through the 'growing pains' of transformation, we can become confused, activated, or irritated. But when we have the right structure, our energy never gets chaotic, because we have the support to help us process and resolve it and we can work effectively towards changing ourselves for the better.

How does your personal world support you in becoming the person you want to be? Who or what clearly supports you in making the right changes in your personal or professional life? One of the reasons some people resist change so much is that they don't have the right support system in place. On some level, they recognize that stepping into change is going to be a slow, difficult process and the potential of getting snagged in one's own process is high without the right support structure.

Just as we need a support system to realize our fullest potential, so too, we need a structure in order to realize our true nature. When we become aware that we are a soul, a spiritual being in a material world, the soul needs a structure to enter into and then, that structure needs to be developed and improved so the soul can thrive within it. So once again, it's important to understand which structure is best-suited for us as we move away from our ego-based-self and closer to the embodiment of our soul-self.

A significant part of the work of transcending the ego-self is knowing how to collapse the structure in which the ego lives—this structure was created long ago and has been reinforced over time. As the ego-structure collapses, the ego becomes fearful—and from its place of fear, it can get us to do all kinds of interesting things if we're not aware of what's going on. If we don't build a structure for the soul-self to thrive in, there is a disconnect, which can lead to emptiness and a lack of fulfillment. Likewise, however, without a structure for the ego, there will be distraction, leading to stress and chaos. Distractions in and of themselves create consequences that we have to resolve, keeping us from dismantling the structure in which the ego has lived. Thus, as we create a structure for our soul-self, we must be mindful of the ego-self, and assuage its fear by being non-judgmental, loving, and accepting of how well it has cared for us over time. When we do this, the ego-self will slowly give way, embrace change, and allow the soul-self supremacy.

Strategy

The third S in the "Triad for Transformation" is the S for "*strategy*" or system. We dealt with aspects of this "S" in the section on "Dealing with Feelings," and here, we'll delve into further features of "strategy"—and how to make it work for you.

Your overall strategy must include a transformational system, just as an entrepreneur or salesperson has a system for growing their business. A specific system defines and establishes everything that needs to be done in a detailed, sequential way. Every mature business person or career professional knows that this is one of the master keys towards achieving success and happiness. They know that without a system in place, they would flounder. Similarly, someone who is interested in transforming themselves must have a system—or they too will flounder.

When working towards transformation, it is crucial to outline a strategy before you begin. The more well-conceived your strategy is and the more effective your transformational system is, the better your chances of success are. One-size-fits-all strategies seldom work; identifying and/or designing a personalized strategy is ideal. The key is deciding what you want. *What are you moving towards?* If you're moving towards something big in your life because you have a bigger goal or a bigger dream, you want to break that dream down into bite-size pieces. Bring it all the way down to that very first piece—that's what you need to focus your energy on. The strategy you design for that first piece will be the strategy that's right for you, right now. It's important too, to be willing to follow through—that will make the difference when it comes to changing yourself and your life.

Choosing a strategy means not just choosing the right one, it also means choosing it at the *right time*—for your soul, not for anybody else's. For example, say you and your coach or mentor are working together and you start developing a strategy for your transformation, a strategy for, say, saving your marriage, or for taking your business to the next level. First, you'll spend a fair amount of time together, and you'll identify, customize, and personalize a strategy (or maybe a set of strategies) that are 100 percent correct for you and your soul, the soul of your business and/or your life, *right here, right now.* That's what makes it so unique and so powerful, because then, when you take that strategy—or those strategies—and apply them to your day-to-day world, you're going to get amazing results, right away.

Let's consider what strategizing might look like in real life. Let's say that someone wants to transform one of their fears—say they are afraid of being vulnerable, they are moving into a new relationship and they want to do things differently this time. Perhaps they have a fear of intimacy, of being abandoned, betrayed, or made wrong. Whatever the fear might be, that fear is activated and it takes over their body and/

or consciousness. The next thing they know, they're thinking: "Maybe this is not the right person…maybe I need to back off…maybe I need to slow down…maybe I need to end this relationship." Any or all of these things might be true, however, what might also be true is that they are anticipating that if they move further in this relationship, something they are afraid of might happen. So, when the person is mindful of all of these scenarios, and they decide that transforming their fear is more important than continuing to allow it to dominate them, strategizing comes into play.

First, they identify the fear, take ownership of it, and then they design a strategy—either on their own or with someone's help. The strategy is 100 percent personalized, customized to acknowledge their fear and where they're at in that point in time. Part of the strategy might be, for example, to open the lines of communication with their partner. Then, they and their partner can agree to cooperate when the fear gets activated. What that process can look like varies: the fearful person might get a timeout, so to speak, and go off to process that fear with the support and understanding of their new partner. Or, perhaps they'll strategize to talk it through. This might happen a number of times, but having a strategy to deal with the fear helps to stop the fear from running the show and influencing the new relationship.

 **Exercises**

For the exercises below, take some quiet time by yourself. Get still. Picture your higher self.

If you don't have an image of your higher self or your soul just yet, picture the words "Higher Self" on the screen of your mind. Place these words right over your heart. With your journal and pen in hand, read these questions. Go with the first answer that comes to you—write it down. Over time, the answers to these questions will change as you change. Be authentic. Stay in the moment—and breathe!

1) Which of the "S's" are you strong in? What about this "S" makes you feel strong?

2) Which of the "S's" are you weak in? What about this "S" makes you feel weak?

3) Which "S" do you feel it would be most beneficial to focus on— or to pay more attention to? Why?

Trust Your Process

I recently came across a note I'd made to myself when a friend and I were struggling through something. All of a sudden, he said, "The will of God will never take you where the grace of God will not protect you." His words helped me to relax immediately into what I was experiencing at that time—they made a huge difference. We do have a choice: we can react to whatever it is that's uncomfortable or scary or we can choose to calm ourselves down and go with it. Once again, we can ride the waves of change like a surfer rides the waves of the ocean. The key is to do our best, to give ourselves permission to let go. Relax into it. Surrender to it. What other option do we have? We can fight it, avoid it, increase our stress, increase our pain and suffering—or we can let go.

How do we know if we're letting go of something? When we're being called to change, the universe or our soul prompts us to move towards something new and different. So, check in with your own higher self, your own inner guidance. Have you been receiving signs that clearly say, "This is what you ought to let go of?" Our higher self will always give us signs. If we're really struggling, we can break it down, take it one step at a time. Remember, our soul has a genuine need to grow and to do that, we must change something within ourselves.

It's powerful to recognize how letting go of something makes space for something new to enter our lives, be it personally, professionally, spiritually, financially, physically, etc.—on any level that we deserve to experience something new in our lives. As spiritual teacher and author Eckhart Tolle says, "Some changes look negative on the surface, but you will soon realize that space is being created in our life for something new to emerge."

We deserve to show up in a new way in our lives. Actually, it's beyond deserving: We are destined to experience life in newer, higher, better, and brighter ways. However, in order for that to happen, we have to let go of relationships, of projects that clearly no longer serve us in our world. Letting go of old ways of thinking and old perceptions in how we've been viewing the world creates space for something new to emerge.

Learning to trust in your higher self is one of the master keys to experiencing true life change on a deep, cellular level. The 37.2 trillion cells in the body have been carrying what we've been hanging onto, and when it is released and resolved, it no longer exists in the cellular structure of the body. We literally feel a shift within the body because our 37 plus trillion cells have restructured themselves to support this change. There's no longer incongruence with that old dynamic that was residing in the cells where we were saying one thing and doing something else. Something happens, we become new and different—from within. Changing on a cellular level creates lasting change!

Just as the body's language is the language of sensation, so too, the higher self draws our attention to the need to change by making us uncomfortable, by creating pain in our lives. Sometimes the pain manifests as unpleasant circumstances, sometimes as physical, emotional, or spiritual difficulties. So, when we trust our higher self, we have to really tap into our experience, and examine our circumstances. If we are in pain, for example, we need to learn to discern between physical and spiritual pain—we need to ask, "Is this pain something I need to go to the doctor for? Is this something I should process or should I simply allow it to happen?" Of course, if a doctor is needed, go to a doctor. If it's processing that's needed, go and process, using whatever transformational system or method you currently use.

We need to train ourselves to think differently about pain and fear. By doing so, it will become easier and more natural to embrace our own process of change as it comes knocking on the door. We have to trust that our higher self has a bigger and better plan in store for us, that the pain we are experiencing might be showing us that we are out of alignment, and that we need to make a shift for our highest good. There's an ebb and flow to life that we cannot always control and may not understand through the limited lens of our five senses when we're letting go of someone or something that's no longer serving us. Many times, this strengthens our inner "trust muscle"—when we're in the process of letting go, we don't see the new that's coming in. In most cases, the new doesn't emerge until we've completely let go of the old. This is why choosing to trust in this higher and greater process is so important. Trust changes everything—by trusting, we can embrace change and succeed in making change. This is why connecting with our higher self can be so beneficial too, it's the part of us that will never forsake us. It's here for us, in all ways, at all times. This is why I said earlier that when change shows up in our lives, we can be assured that our soul is already on board. That said, it's up to us to connect with our soul or higher self and then to honor that connection by trusting the voice of our soul. It'll change our life for the better, forever.

Will you choose to trust in the process of your higher self? You'll make and remake this choice many times along the way. When you're going through it, your doubts and insecurities can creep in. You might find yourself asking: "Will this ever end? How much more is there? Will I make it? Why is it taking so long?" Remember, your soul is on board, the act of trusting can help you to relax as you experience change.

Letting Go When It's Time

Recognizing that letting go is a process and trusting that the process will unfold at the right time can really help us to embrace change. Letting go always happens in its own time and with its own rhythm. And, it can be a deep, long process when we're letting go of something we've held onto for a long time: a cherished dream, a hoped-for career, an anticipated business accomplishment, or a long-term relationship with a loved one. So, when you are in the process, have faith—there is a light at the end of the tunnel!

Not long ago, I had just returned home from a road trip when I noticed that my deck was in need of a good scrubbing. The next morning, as I was cleaning, I noticed something on the upper exterior part of the screen door. I touched it. It felt like a snail, but looked like some kind of bug, about ½ inch in diameter. Intending to escort it to the other side of the deck, I placed my fingers gently around it. But, it wasn't going to move without me applying more pressure. I knew that if I applied more pressure it would probably die so I let it stay on the screen. For the next two days, I went out to check on my little friend, to find it in the exact same place. On the third morning, the little creature was gone without a trace. Whether it flew away or crawled away, I don't know. What I do know is that when it was done with its process, when it had gone through whatever it was going through, it let go of the screen and moved on.

Deeper changes take time; your transformation will be a process. There is no such thing as a "quick fix." Transformation on a deep level is unsettling. Sometimes it's a question of sitting with it, without reacting. Perhaps we're meant to be exactly where we are right now. We don't always have to be moving forward. At times, we might be better served to just be with what's happening, instead of trying to make it go away or hurrying the process so we can get on the other side and feel happy again. There is an "other side," we will feel lighter, and we will feel free and happy again—perhaps more than we ever were before.

 **Exercises**

For the exercises below, take some quiet time by yourself. Get still. Picture your higher self.

If you don't have an image of your higher self or your soul just yet, picture the words "Higher Self" on the screen of your mind. Place these words right over your heart. With your journal and pen in hand, read these questions. Go with the first answer that comes to you—write it down. Over time, the answers to these questions will change as you change. Be authentic. Stay in the moment—and breathe!

1) What are you in the process of letting go of right now?

2) Is the timing right for you to let this go now?

3) How do you know you're ready to let this go now?

4) Would it be beneficial for you to be more trusting in the process of letting this go? If so, where, with whom, or in what way could you be more trusting?

Get Ready to Change!

As mentioned earlier, when it comes to embracing change, we have to be ready and willing to actually step into what we're changing. Sometimes we're not yet aware of just how ready we are for change but if we start declaring out loud, "I am ready and willing to make this change," we truly become ready to change. We also become more trusting in the change process. The process can also be a little easier if we take the time to reconnect with the part of us that's influencing the change. If, for example, a change is in our highest and best interest, then the impetus to change is coming from our soul. As we recognize this and tap into our soul, we draw strength from it, it empowers us to walk consciously through the change process. We stop resisting, we surrender totally to change, and we embrace all new challenges that come our way, for we know that ultimately, they will lead us to a rewarding, fulfilling life.

Transformation as a Lifestyle

When we stop resisting, we end our suffering and unnecessary pain. This is the beginning of actualizing our true soul-self potential. Once we turn our transformation into a lifestyle, we relax into change. We surrender to it. We go with it. When we're no longer creating unnecessary suffering, our transformation accelerates. So, rather than trying to get rid of your feelings when the ego and your fear become activated, rather than freezing up, breathe through it. It'll likely reveal itself in the pit of your stomach. Relax into it, rather than resist it. Your motto could be: *Breathe—and keep going.*

Should we choose to let ourselves completely feel our feelings and our fear, they will pass through us. Remember the mantra, *Relax, Surrender, and Let Go.* As we begin to trust in the natural process of transformation, we embrace whatever we're currently going through as it unfolds. We breathe into its promise of expanded opportunity.

 **Exercises**

For the exercises below, take some quiet time by yourself. Get still. Picture your higher self.

If you don't have an image of your higher self or your soul just yet, picture the words "Higher Self" on the screen of your mind. Place these words right over your heart. With your journal and pen in hand, read these questions. Go with the first answer that comes to you—write it down. Over time, the answers to these questions will change as you change. Be authentic. Stay in the moment—and breathe!

1) When was the last time you said these powerful words to yourself: "Relax, Surrender, and Let Go?"

2) When was the last time you took a deep, slow breath?

3) Is it in your highest and best interests to turn transformation into a lifestyle? If not, why not? If so, why?

4) Have you been resisting your own transformation lately? And, if you have, could you just embrace it? How might it serve you and your life, if you were to embrace it, full-on? How much energy does it take to resist? What would happen if you truly let go, once and for all, of that old need to resist change?

Breathe!

Breathing is so important when it comes to transformational experiences. It helps to develop a habit of checking in with your breath ten times a day. Make a note to yourself that says, "Breathe." Post it somewhere you can see it often throughout the day. It will serve as a reminder until taking a deep, slow breath ten times a day becomes a way of life.

Make a note to yourself that says, "Breathe."

As soon as we become afraid of anyone or anything, the first thing that happens is that we forget to breathe. We're not likely even aware that we're holding our breath—sometimes for as long as thirty to sixty seconds—or that our body has become tight. That tightness is letting us know we're in the state of unconscious resistance that we talked about earlier, whereby we tighten up as way to protect ourselves from what we think or perceive is happening to us. Many times, our thinking—the way we're perceiving what we're experiencing in the moment—can be distorted. Sometimes it's as simple as remembering to take a conscious breath and choosing to relax into that tense energy.

When we're in our change process, there's a good chance that we're either breathing shallowly or we're holding our breath. As soon as we become afraid of anyone or anything—and change can certainly be a fear-inducing experience—we forget to breathe.

Our breath carries transformational properties. Oxygen quiets the mind, improves concentration, energizes the nervous system, and promotes healing. As we learn how to breathe correctly, breathe deeply, and breathe more slowly, the healing benefits of oxygen are drawn into the body. Should you find yourself feeling stressed or anxious, take five deep breaths through your nostrils.

We breathe from the diaphragm naturally when we're breathing through the nose. The diaphragm stimulates our parasympathetic nervous system, which can help calm us down. Chest breathing stimulates the sympathetic nervous system which can trigger a flight, flight, or freeze reaction in the body. So, as you move through the trials and triumphs of each day—remember to breathe! The calmer you are when going through a change, the easier answering the call to change will be.

The Practices in the next chapter are designed to help you meet the challenges of today's busy and stressful lifestyle—do any one of these practices every day for thirty days, and you'll find yourself developing transformational habits and making changes that will serve you well in your life.

 **Exercises**

For the exercises below, take some quiet time by yourself. Get still. Picture your higher self.

If you don't have an image of your higher self or your soul just yet, picture the words "Higher Self" on the screen of your mind. Place these words right over your heart. With your journal and pen in hand, read these questions. Go with the first answer that comes to you—write it down. Over time, the answers to these questions will change as you change. Be authentic. Stay in the moment—and breathe!

1) What transformational process or system do you use? How does it help you?

2) What would it do for you—or what *does* it do for you—to have someone support you along your transformational path?

3) What makes a great transformational teacher or coach? What are the three most important qualities you want in a teacher or coach?

4) How could a coach or teacher help you in your life (personally or professionally) right now?

CHAPTER 13
TWELVE TRANSFORMATIONAL PRACTICES

The Law of Accumulation says that a small thing, accumulated over time, can become a big thing. So, when we apply this law to our transformational practice, it's what we practice every day that really counts. What we practice daily over time accumulates in the effect it has on our life. If the practice is positive over time, it will strengthen us and change our lives for the better. The same holds true if a practice is negative—over time, it weakens us and changes our lives for the worse.

In this chapter, you'll find a series of twelve practices that you can choose from to practice every day. Select at least one and practice it every day for at least thirty days. Then, choose another one to add to your daily routine and practice it every day for thirty days. Transforming our lives is like developing our muscles. If we are just starting out lifting weights at the gym, for example, we decide what part of our body we are going to focus on first. Then, we gradually expand our focus to other parts of our body and so on. We can apply that same principle here—only what we are developing now are our inner muscles.

You'll know which of these practices is right for you to bring into your life by where you are at, right now. Choose the one that resonates most with you—and stick with it for thirty days. You'll be astounded at the changes that take place in you—and in your life—in just one short month. Get ready to transform!

Envision Your Best Self.

As we tap in and consistently hold a greater vision of ourselves, we begin to move towards this vision. The vision in and of itself serves as a sort of tractor beam. As the vision is created and we place our focus on it, the vision pulls us toward itself.

In this practice, envision your future best self, a month from now, maybe even a year from now. Imagine what your improved life looks like and feels like. Focus all of your attention on your better, future self. Remember, whatever or wherever your intention goes, energy flows. Ask yourself, "When I reflect on my life and where I want it to go, what does my improved life look like?" Whatever your answer is, that's what you connect to. For example, perhaps your future, better life includes a romantic relationship, or enriched interactions with your children, expansion in an aspect of your financial life, or a new development in your career, your business life, or your health—whatever it looks like to you, connect to that future best self.

The key here, of course, is to be able to see it happening. While you see it happening on the screen of your mind, also feel this visualization in your body. Feel it as if it is happening right now. This is a powerful practice, especially if you are doing it every day. Once you create a vision that is right for you, the practice can be done in a couple of minutes or less. The key is to do it every day.

This practice of envisioning your best self can also be used in other ways to enhance your life. For example, say you have been unwell. You can visualize getting on the other side of the experience, imagining your future health as you wish it to be. Similarly, if you are in the process of moving your home, visualize yourself on the other side of the move, tap into how you wish to feel in your new place. In the same way, you can apply this practice to your day-to-day relationships. Say, for example, you are about to enter into an uncomfortable conversation with someone who is really important to you and the idea stresses you out a bit. Simply visualize yourself on the other side of the conversation. Feel in your body the way you would like to feel after the discussion is over.

This is a powerful practice, and, as you can see, it can be utilized each and every day to make an enormous difference in your life.

Do the Thing You are Afraid of Doing.

When you do something you are afraid of doing, you begin to recognize fear as an invitation to change. You must ask yourself, "Am I done with letting fear play with me and my life?" When you do things you fear, when you take action, you create a better situation for yourself, forever. This is *divine right action.*

So many people are looking to connect with their divine self. Yet, a lot of people have not yet realized that a part of connecting with the divine is identifying the thing that they have been afraid of doing. So, whatever that is for you, make a decision. Step into it—do the thing you have been afraid to do. I love what author Michael Singer has to say on fear in his book, *The Untethered Soul:*

> *Fear is the cause of every problem. It's the root of all prejudices and the negative emotions of anger, jealousy, and possessiveness. If you had no fear, you could be perfectly happy...You'd be willing to face everything and everyone.*

As a daily practice, you could ask yourself, "If there is something I am afraid of doing today, what is it?" Whatever your answer is, check to see if you can make the decision right now, to do that very thing today.

The key with this practice is being willing to get started—and then, once you have started, to keep going. It is wise to plan that the fear-based ego, at some point, will get activated. It's going to happen, it is just a question of time. So, when it does, you want to feel that energy. You know it will be fear-rooted, so be ready to feel it in the pit of your stomach. You'll feel it in the "fear belt," that part of your body that runs across the upper part of the solar plexus. Imagine the transverse colon, it runs from the right side of the body to the left side of the body—that area is often referred to as the "fear belt." When fear gets activated, more than likely you are going to feel an energy rising in that part of your body.

As you feel this fear in the pit of your stomach, or in the belt of fear, stay conscious of the fear, let yourself feel it while you breathe into it, but no matter what, keep going.

The fact that you are noticing your fear is huge. It has been activated, it is a direct result of your choice to do the thing you have been afraid of. But as you keep going, through the fear, it will begin to clear. It is only when you stop and engage in one of your old strategies (as in "power em," or "stuff em") that the fear becomes stronger.

So, ultimately, once we identify the thing that is most right for us to do, the next step is facing our fears. Here is something I have found helpful. If you don't want to do something, don't do it. But don't stop because you are afraid of doing it. If you do, remember, you are always working with the Law of Accumulation, whether your actions are negative or positive. If you don't work with your fear, that fear will get stronger, and over time, it can play havoc in your life. It can even begin to paralyze you, restricting you in moving your life forward. But if you do the thing you are afraid of doing, you will overcome the fear—and fly.

Release Your Thoughts onto Paper.

Journaling is a great transformational practice for releasing our thoughts and our feelings—especially those thoughts and feelings that repeat over and over again. It is a simple, yet highly beneficial practice and it can be done anywhere, any time. We just have to be willing to do it. I say "willing" because when we are really in our stuff, that's when we won't want to do it. Here's a ten-minute exercise: Grab your pen and note pad. Without analyzing or judging, write down everything you are currently thinking and feeling for ten minutes. You'll be amazed!

If we muster up the oomph to start writing out our thoughts and feelings as they come to us, we will be amazed at how this simple act can get our energy moving. Of course, once the energy of those repetitive thoughts, stuck feelings, or stagnant emotions starts moving, we come back to our center and begin to calm down.

Get Everything Moving.

Without conscious movement, energy becomes sticky, heavy, and/or stuck. We need to understand how important the movement of all four of our bodies—physical, mental, emotional, or spiritual—really is. When our energy gets stuck, it automatically moves us away from our center. It pops us out of our natural self.

When our energy gets stuck, it moves us away from our center.

For example, if we become emotionally stuck, if we haven't consciously done anything to move our emotions, if we suppressed our feelings instead of releasing them, that holds us back from doing what we want to do in our lives. As a being, we are energy, and our energy wants to move! If you can't access your energy because it is stuck, or backed up, or sticky, it will end up using you. Should you find yourself feeling stuck or victimized by things that are happening, do a reset—with intention. Take some action, engage the moving centers in your body.

What might that look like? Say you are emotionally stuck, for example, something has happened and you feel victimized. Perhaps someone said something to you or didn't understand you. Get authentic. Reach out to that other person, be a little vulnerable (even if it's scary!), have a conversation with the intention of getting a reality check. What happened from their point of view?

In such a situation, people can make the mistake of only talking about themselves, their hurts, what was done to them, how it made them feel, and so on. It doesn't dawn on them to turn the table a little bit. Does that other person have something of value to contribute to the conversation? Maybe the person made a mistake, maybe they admit they were wrong. Next thing you know, your energy shifts and starts to move again because it has been acknowledged properly, you did something to move the energy. You feel lighter, freer, you are speaking more truth, in an authentic, conscious, responsible way to this person—and they are responding in kind.

If a person is right for you in your life, then they want the same thing you want, they want the energy between you to flow. It doesn't feel good to them when the energy gets stuck, either. Even if it is just you holding the stuck energy, if they are genuine, more than likely, they feel it anyway, even though they might not be able to put their finger on what is up. The moment you reach out, make the call, have the conversation, the energy starts moving—not just for you, but for them as well.

When we are conscious of this practice, and we are willing and ready to engage in getting everything moving, we can identify the right kind of action to take—and then, take it!

Getting everything moving can be just about moving the energy in the body, doing something physical, with intention. When we get moving, many toxins are carried to the lungs to be eliminated in the respiratory system. When doing something physical, if we can work up a good sweat, all the better; sweating facilitates the release of toxins through the skin. Maybe we recognize that we feel low or heavy, and we realize we have to clear stuck energy. A visit to the acupuncturist, a trip to the gym, getting on a bicycle and riding around the park, going to the pool, jumping in the ocean or a lake, moving your body—sometimes that is all you need to do to get the energy moving. Or maybe hiking or dancing is what you like to do to clear dense energy. Sometimes it can be as simple as cleaning your house or garage. You can turn cleaning into an open-eyed meditation. Once you are fully engaged in cleaning, something starts to happen, the trapped energy in the body starts to move, and you start to feel lighter and freer again. Why? Because energy is moving.

Check for Needy Energy.

Earlier, I talked about the needy self and needy energy. Checking for needy energy daily can be a huge transformational practice. Remember, needy energy—or rather the *needs* within needy energy—are much like weeds in our garden. Perhaps we have a need to be defensive, a need to be liked, a need to look good, a need to be right, whatever. If we just go into the garden once in a while and weed, no matter how many weeds we pluck, thirty days from now, or three months from now, there will be more weeds in our garden. But when we pull these needy energy 'weeds' up on a daily basis, we come to a place where they are no longer overwhelming or controlling us, they do not have the same influence or hold over us anymore.

For example, perhaps by integrating this practice into a daily routine, you might discover that you have a need to be defensive. It's not that we should never defend what's right, but when our defensiveness comes from our ego-self, we might discover that each time we engage with that need to be defensive, we push someone or something away from us. That creates more pain or more suffering—and, as noted earlier, it creates *unnecessary* pain.

As you get in touch with your need to be defensive, you might discover that a lot of people around you are defensive. Perhaps you have looked at others in certain situations and said, "Wow, why are you being so defensive?" But now, you slow it down a little bit, and you notice a pattern—everywhere you go, somehow, some way, you spot it—people being defensive. You are slowly becoming aware that even though others can be defensive around you, it is *you, your ego, your needy self* that is being defensive.

So, as you go through your day, keep checking for needy energy. Before you go into a meeting, before you enter an uncomfortable conversation, before you step into a project or activity, check yourself for needy energy. Just pose these questions, "If there was a need influencing this activity, what might that be? Is it a need to be right? A need for attention? A need for recognition? A need to be heard? A need for something else?" Whatever you are thinking of doing, check in. It's possible to get caught up in the stress of it all, trying to achieve those goals, checking things off on our To Do list.

It is not that we shouldn't have goals, but if we get caught up in trying too hard to achieve those goals because we're needy for something (whether we're aware of it or not), we'll end up sabotaging something. Some people have gotten so caught up, they have forgotten to live their lives. They sometimes begin to feel that they don't even have a life anymore.

What is amazing about taking time to check in with your needy energy is that nine times out of ten, the energy is sitting right on the surface, waiting to be recognized, acknowledged, or brought into conscious awareness. And when you spot it once, then you see it repeatedly, in full, living color. You see it, you feel it. Sometimes it amazes you, sometimes it shocks you, sometimes you are pleasantly surprised. Sometimes, you think, "Wow, I had no idea that my ego created this needy energy that influences the way I'm showing up in the world."

Once you become aware of this needy energy, you have done fifty percent of the transformational work around it. By recognizing it, it no longer has such power over you, it doesn't have the same influence— simply see it and the transformational magic comes into play.

Unless we see it, we can't clear it. Until you see it in your own day-to-day life, you can't clear it.

Take Twenty Minutes for Silence or to Go Within.

Commonly, when the ego is faced with taking the time for silence each day, it says, "There is no time! I have too many things to do! There is no time to go within, no time for silence." Now, this practice only calls for twenty minutes out of an entire period of twenty-four hours. Twenty minutes!

People sometimes laugh when I mention this in my seminars. We have just ended a meditation. They went inward for twenty minutes, and it dawns on them that because they do not take time in their busy lives to be silent, they lose their objectivity, they become fully subjective. And the next thing they know, they are under the influence of their ego—and the ego has something to say: "There is no time!" So, it is easy for people to justify, mentally, why I don't need to take the twenty minutes, why I don't have to go within, why I don't need to practice being silent. I simply don't have any time—and furthermore, I have all these things on my list that I'm already running behind on!

This is a great trick of the ego, isn't it?

This is a great trick of the ego, isn't it? When you take twenty minutes out of your busy day to move into silence or to go within, you actually gain time, because you get more efficient, clearer, calmer—and you do things soulfully.

So, what might this practice look like for you? It might be as simple as reading an inspirational book first thing in the morning as a way to start your day, sitting on a park bench during your lunch hour, or doing a formal meditation practice in the evening. When we allow ourselves to slow down every day, get connected with our true soul essence, and calm down, over time, it has a hugely positive effect on every part of our lives. It helps us to catch things that are going on in our lives that we would never catch otherwise because we are moving too quickly.

I'm not saying we shouldn't move fast from time to time, to get a lot of things done. But when we get caught up in doing doing doing; busy busy busy; gotta go gotta go; we risk disconnecting from ourselves, moving away from our soul center. If that goes unchecked, somewhere along the way, something will happen—in a relationship with someone dear to us, something in our financial life, etc. But if we take twenty minutes every day to slow down, if we connect with what is going on within us, we connect with our higher selves. We start to become aware of a subtle inner awareness. Perhaps our higher self is giving us a message, or prompting us to do something—go left, turn right; change a decision we've made; or step in and make a decision—whatever it might be.

However and whenever you do this practice, you'll find it powerful—because you are "on purpose" now. And, once you start, it becomes important for your soul to take time for silence on a day-to-day basis.

Decide on Up to Three Things You Will Accomplish Today.

There are two aspects to this practice. The first is to identify three things that you want to do today—and to include in those three things one activity that you would be willing to do that you know would be uncomfortable for you.

The second part of the practice is to *do* these three things. This practice can super-charge our lives and move us forward on every level—personally, professionally, financially, spiritually, and relationship-wise.

Keep it to three things. Some people put twelve things on their list, but this is a recipe for increased levels of anxiety and increased levels of stress—both of which are forms of unconscious resistance. When there are too many things on the list, there is a real possibility we can get distracted, doing things that we have no business doing, instead of doing things we should be doing.

Another group of people won't operate with a list—what they want to accomplish today doesn't dawn on them, they just do what's in front of them—and get scattered in the process.

Somewhere between those people with twelve things on their list and those with no list at all, is another group that has a list, but avoids doing uncomfortable things. Some of these folks can even become addicted to doing only those things that are comfortable for them.

It's not bad to do only comfortable things *per se*, but when we get into this habit, there isn't a lot of growth or healing, or any opportunities to learn lessons. But when we do something uncomfortable, magic happens, we give ourselves a great gift. I know it doesn't look like a gift but doing uncomfortable things can be a powerful practice in moving our lives forward.

American writer Mark Twain once said, "Eat a live frog first thing in the morning and nothing worse will happen to you the rest of the day." One of my most beloved and respected mentors, public speaker Brian Tracy, took it further and wrote a wonderful book on that premise entitled, *Eat That Frog!* Throughout his career, Tracy discovered—and rediscovered—a simple truth. He says that the ability to concentrate single-mindedly on your most important task, to do it well, and to finish it completely is the key to great success, achievement, respect, status, and happiness in life.

The idea is that each morning, if you complete a task that you would most likely procrastinate on, then you can go about your day knowing you did it—and the rest of your day will be easy in comparison. Let's say it's writing an uncomfortable letter or email to someone, dealing with an upset customer, calling someone you're intimidated by, following up on old calls, making calls to new prospects, or cleaning out the garage or the storage bin. Whatever it is, once you've gotten that dreadful task out of the way, the rest of your day flows—because what other task could be more uncomfortable than the one you just completed? It's a simple technique and yet so powerful. You ate the frog!

So, when should you decide what the "Up to three things you intend to do each day" are? You can wait until you get up in the morning and decide. That's okay. But, even better, take a few minutes to make this decision the night before, when you are getting ready for bed—get really clear on it, make a written list. And, if you really want to grow, stretch, heal, or expand yourself as a soul, put one thing on your list that will be uncomfortable.

When you do this the night before, here is what happens—you are in-putting this To-Do list into your subconscious self. This is the part of you that never sleeps, the part of you that works 24/7. You give the subconscious mind a command, and your subconscious starts working while you sleep. When you wake up in the morning, your subconscious has given you a running start, so you are even more effective, you have more power to get these one to three things done in the course of the day. With your subconscious mind on your team, you'll be productive, creative, and inspired!

Be Willing to Experience the Uncomfortable.

Neale Donald Walsch once said that life begins at the end of your comfort zone. When we leave our comfort zone, good, positive things happen. We heal, change, and grow to the exact degree to which we are willing to feel uncomfortable. This is where spiritual enlightenment is found, where it is most uncomfortable to be. So, ultimately, this practice is about expanding our relationship to pain.

As noted earlier, when we were kids, our bodies were changing and growing and we experienced "growing pains." Just as we are all destined to grow from children into adults, we are all destined to grow and expand into a better life. Yet, if we resist the uncomfortable part of the growth process, we will hold ourselves back from having a better life. So, if we want to grow our career, our business, and/or our significant relationships, we have to "embrace the uncomfortable."

So, ask yourself, "If there was something that I might be uncomfortable doing, but that I am truly supposed to be doing, what might that be?" Whatever your answer, can you make the decision right now that you are just simply going to do it? Everything in life comes down to a decision. We choose how we are going to show up in the world, and we have free will to choose everything we do. So, recognizing that if we want to grow, we have to do uncomfortable things, and then consciously choosing to do them is an act of bravery.

It takes courage to heal, it takes courage to change, and it takes courage to grow. When we choose to step into "the uncomfortable," it builds inner strength, it raises our self-esteem, and it increases our self-confidence. *Ready...Set...Grow!*

Chunking Things Down. (or Breaking Things Down)

When we become overwhelmed, it is often because something new or unexpected is coming at us and we are not breaking the information down properly. For example, say we get a speeding ticket—we were not planning on it and yet there it is. So, the question becomes, "What next?" What happens to us internally? What do we go through?

Usually, we are shocked. Then, reality makes its way into our awareness. It might take a couple of days to accept it, but soon, we relax into our bodies and make peace with the speeding ticket. Then, we need to decide again, "What next?" Are we going to pay the ticket, go to court and fight it, or take a driver's program to reduce the points on our license? What is our strategy going to be?

In the process of deciding, we are breaking our problem down into manageable parts or "chunks." We are literally "chunking it down." Whether we are moving towards accomplishing our goals, checking things off of our To Do list, navigating life's challenges, or dealing with our own activated energy, the "Chunking it Down" strategy is a key for transformation.

If we are not properly breaking down the energy of these kinds of situations, we may begin to feel stressed, stuck, or snagged. And, once stuck, we can start to feel overwhelmed. If we get stressed, we might start pushing back—against a situation or against another person. This, of course, in turn activates our unconscious resistance. Then, we can get into full-on pushing mode—we might not even be aware we are doing it. So, we need a strategy.

The best strategy to deal with these stressful situations is to "chunk things down" properly, to break down what is showing up for us.

First, we need to check our body for unconscious resistance. If it is there, it will show itself as a tight or tense energy in the body. To check in and clear unconscious resistance, take a quiet moment out. Slow things down a little. Take five breaths through your nostrils and bring your attention to your throat area. Feel for any tight or tense energy there. Do the same with the center of your chest as well as your solar plexus. Should you discover tight energy in any of these three areas, this is your body's way of telling you that you are in unconscious resistance.

It is difficult to break something down in our lives when we are in resistance. Resistance is a fighting energy—we are fighting with our own energy. So, if any one of these three areas are tight (if two or more are tight, then choose one area to focus on), place your attention on that area. As you do, relax into that area. You might think of this as giving up the fight you are in with your own energy. As you give up the fight, as you surrender and let the energy be what it is, it starts to loosen and release. Use the mantra: "Relax, surrender, and let go."

To learn more about this strategy, please visit the section on The TransCovery Process® at *www.DaleHalaway.com*

Identifying and clearing resistance is a critical part of the strategy of "chunking down" whatever is activating us. Again, remember, *what we resist persists*—meaning that what we resist, block, or avoid will only become stronger.

Now, the second part of the "chunking it down" strategy is to organize the issues that have arisen for you in order of their importance.

Then, chunk each one down. What needs to be done and when? Who will be responsible for getting those things done? You'll know when you've truly released your unconscious resistance because you'll start to feel more relaxed in your own body. Again: "Relax, surrender, and let go."

There is a direct connection between how we break things down in our lives and how our body breaks things down. We take in food which then turns on the body's digestive system. The body breaks down our food and absorbs the nutrients. When we are stressed, we can start creating digestive problems, and when the body is not digesting food properly, we can get indigestion. This is the body's way of letting us know something is off. If this goes on for a while, it's just a question of time, we are going to start having physical problems. We can get so jammed up, we can't take anything in or deal with the things on our To Do list. Similarly, if we are not dealing with life's problems correctly, if we are not chunking things down properly, it can create other problems in our lives.

I have often found that when someone hasn't been dealing with life's problems or challenges properly, they have digestive issues. It's literally the Law of Correspondence at play: *As within, so without.* But, when we change or correct what is going on inside, it will naturally begin to correct things on the outside—and vice versa. When we learn to chunk things down, we begin to show up differently—and we produce new, different, and positive results in our lives.

Trust That Whatever is Changing is Changing for the Better.

There is a higher, divine power at play when we are in the process of changing. Of course, when we are in this process, it can be difficult for us to see the higher power. This is a principal reason that it can be beneficial for us to have someone "in our corner"—someone to support us. A transformational life coach, a counselor, a psychologist—someone who is really there to support us—can be further along on the path, they can be clearer, they can maintain a level of objectivity, and they can see the divine at play.

Of course, as we dive deeper into a change process, as we move from being objective about our lives to being subjective, we can't see the truth of what is really occurring. But remember, there is tremendous freedom when we accept *what is*. It loosens up the attachments we have to those people or things we should let go of. This is what opens the doorway to new directions and experiences. It's a choice to trust that there's someone better coming into our life, or to trust that there's a better way to grow our business. It's a choice to trust that there's a better career just waiting for us as we're transitioning from the one that's no longer working.

When our lives are being shaken up, we might ask, "Is there something bigger going on here? Is it possible that what's happening right now is exactly what's supposed to be happening? Am I to go on a relationship fast, or a career fast for a while? If so, can I just accept what's happening right now? Can I surrender to the resistance or stress I have around whatever is happening?" It does not help to resist or to be stressed about whatever is happening around or within us in any event, that only makes whatever we are going through more painful!

If you choose to integrate this practice into your day-to-day life, you will learn how to let go. You'll soon let go of everything you can't control and consciously choose to embrace those things you can control.

Be Gentle with Yourself and the Process You are Going Through.

Whenever we are hard on ourselves, it makes whatever we are experiencing more difficult. Beating ourselves up or making ourselves wrong when the going gets rough brings our growth to a halt. As soon as we become aware of what we are doing, we can choose consciously to be gentle with ourselves and whatever it is that we're going through.

What does this look like? Say we go on a food binge, for example, or we show up late for a meeting, or skip a workout—instead of blaming or judging ourselves, can we give ourselves permission to simply be okay with it? If we can, instead of our energy getting stuck, our energy keeps moving.

We can also engage this 'self-care' practice with others. Perhaps we are being too hard on our kids, for example, or on our wife, husband, or partner. If we realize that this is what we are doing, we can ask ourselves, "Is this serving me, or serving those in this relationship that are so dear to me?" Similarly, you can ask yourself this question about your relationship with yourself: "Does it serve me to be so hard on myself? Might it be better if I were more gentle with myself?"

Truly, it can never serve us to be hard on ourselves in any transformational process we are going through. The process itself is uncomfortable enough! To make it wrong, or to make ourselves wrong, is to simply increase our own discomfort. Be gentle with yourself—and be gentle with others.

Now, I'm not saying you should be passive with everyone around you. There are times when it is appropriate to speak up to someone in a firm, conscious, responsible, and mature way. But that is not what this practice calls for. This practice calls us to take a look at how we are with others, how we are with ourselves, each and every day. It calls us to recognize that how we are with others and how we are with ourselves has an effect on our lives. That effect can be positive or negative—it all depends on how we choose to show up in our day-to-day world.

Celebrate the Victory!

When someone experiences a victory and they take a moment to really feel what it's like to accomplish something, it promotes a state of wellbeing. Whether any accomplishment is minor or major—it is important to acknowledge and celebrate positive events in our lives.

Celebrating victories is not 'on the radar' of people who are focused on the negative. They neither acknowledge nor celebrate their successes—they don't even see them. Sometimes, someone might ask them about a significant event—and it stumps them. Their achievement hasn't been their focus—they've been focusing on what they didn't attain, not on what they did attain.

The Law of Increase says: *That which we praise, increases.* If we turn the conscious act of praising or celebrating our victories into a day-to-day practice, we find ourselves experiencing more wins in our lives. Similarly, if we focus on our losses, we experience more loss. The Law of Increase does not care how we use it. If we use this law incorrectly, we lose. If we use it correctly, we gain. It is that simple.

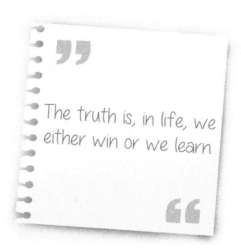

The truth is, in life, we either win or we learn.

Some people believe that in the 'game of life', we either win, or we lose. The truth is, in life, we either win or we learn. The winning days are the days in which our confidence builds and strengthens. The learning days are the days in which we are presented with the transformational opportunity to heal, learn, and expand. When we lose, there is something to heal from, to learn from, and to grow from. You see, if we adopt the attitude that there are no bad experiences in life, but only opportunities for personal and spiritual growth, we can look for the growth in all bad or painful experiences in our lives. If we seek the opportunities for growth and expansion in everything, we will find it.

So, at the end of each day, our self-talk question ought to be, "Was this a learning day or was this a winning day?" We genuinely need both types of days in our lives. We need losses to help us grow and learn, and we need our victories to inspire us to move forward.

In my coaching work, I have everybody work with a victory journal. It is startling how many people feel challenged by working with a victory journal. For example, we'll be starting a session and I'll ask the client to read their victory journal entries from the previous week. They'll tell me all the reasons they never got to it. Many people just can't take five or ten minutes to write down a victory they experienced in the week prior. When challenged about this, they may see that a good percentage of their focus has been on the negative, on what they don't have and what is not working, instead of what they do have and what is working. But at some point, they begin to make the transition, they transition from the inside out, they shift their internal focus. What was focused on the negative becomes focused on the positive. Now, not only do they journal their victories, they look forward to speaking their victories out loud. Speaking your victories out loud is good for the soul!

CHAPTER 14

FINDING YOUR DIVINE SELF

Being called to change is ultimately about finding your way back home, finding the truest version of you—*the real you*. It is a call to return back to your natural state, back to who you really are—and you are divine.

Everything the Divine is...you are!

When you find your way back to your true self, you feel comfortable in your own skin, you feel whole and complete, you have moments when you feel a deep sense of connection to yourself and to the world. Even though you may not be able to sustain that connection, you know it's real because you have experienced it. Once you get a glimpse of this, in an experiential way, you can no longer deny who you truly are, and what you are a part of. This will certainly change things, it will remind you of what it's like to be connected with your divine self. It will inspire you to do more of what really matters in your life and will engender a deep sense of self-appreciation and self-love. If we make being in love with the person we are becoming our new barometer, then how we're living our life, what we're doing, and those we're hanging out with can serve as our measuring system as we move towards expressing our truest selves.

As we begin to do what makes us happy naturally, it's important to notice what arises. Positive and negative emotions, ways of thinking, and states of being can begin to surface. All of these have value. For example, perhaps a negative emotional response we have more often than we might wish originates in our past. If we can access it without judging ourselves as being bad or wrong, the experience can support us in learning a life lesson. Similarly, a positive emotional response likely has something to do with healing or clearing our core issues.

On the path to finding ourselves, we need to recognize that perhaps we lost ourselves somewhere along the way and that it's time, if we haven't done so already, to find our way back home. It's from this place of *being our true self* that we can bring a slice of heaven into our day-to-day lives.

How often do you express your true self? How easy or natural is it for you? Is there someone in your life to whom you can express your true self easily?

Most people put on a mask or have a specific persona depending upon different situations. When was the last time you put a mask on and tried to be something or someone other than your real self in order to be accepted, liked, or loved?

By choosing to be authentic, we share the truth of who we really are.

Remember the ego: when under the unconscious influence of the needy ego-self, we might find ourselves becoming one of the personas we have created. When we commit to expressing our true soul-self, however, we'll catch and purge our needy energy. By consciously choosing to be more trusting of others and by allowing ourselves to be authentic in interaction with others, it becomes easy for us to simply share the truth of who we really are.

The Power of Change

A quote attributed to Mahatma Gandhi says, "Be the change you wish to see in the world." That's the promise: the change we seek, we can become. Who do we genuinely want to become? If we want to see better parenting in the world, for example, substantial numbers of us must transform into the best parents we can be in our own personal lives. If we want to see real, authentic leaders in the world, first we need to become real authentic leaders in our own lives. How do we lead others in our own lives? How do we lead ourselves?

This is where real-world transformation exists: it happens within our selves, one life at a time. As more of us step up and take full responsibility for our own growth and wellbeing, we bring greater change to the way we are as a human race. If we wait for someone else to make changes in their life, or we wait for someone to come into our lives and make changes for us, we'll be waiting a long time. This is what most of our society has been doing: waiting. This hasn't worked. Blaming others when the changes we seek haven't come about doesn't help to advance our humanity, either. It keeps us repeating the same old issues. Doing something repeatedly that's clearly no longer working doesn't make it work any better. In order to make the world a better place, we have to take responsibility for our lives and our realities, including our own personal transformation, growth, and wellbeing.

Remember some of the life-transforming questions you asked yourself earlier? Ask these questions again: "If there is something I am being called to change right now in my life, what might that be? If there is some part of my past that I should be healing or resolving, what might that be? If I knew I had the power to change something for the better in my life, would I use it? If I could become a catalyst for others to make changes in their lives, would I?" And, here's the key question: *"Am I ready to transform?"*

As mentioned earlier, we can completely transform our lives, we have the inner power to do so. But how many people on our planet act as if they don't have the power to make life changes? Instead, they complain about their problems, repeating the same mistakes over and over again, all the while blaming and judging others. All this strategy does is amplify their problems.

Perhaps we're afraid to change because of what change implies. Perhaps we have to let go of our need to control, to play it safe, to protect ourselves. But, we have to ask, "Protect ourselves from what?" "What's really going on here?" Most importantly, we have to ask, "How is holding on to these needs or fears working so far?" Put it to the test: A deeper question might be, *"What are we so afraid of?"* Are we afraid that we will make a mistake, lose respect, be made wrong, and ultimately be rejected? Some people make sure they never fail or get rejected. They are always in a protective and controlling mode. It takes tremendous energy to maintain this stance. Of course, nobody wants to fail or be rejected. But holding onto our fear will only cause us to become so preoccupied with avoiding failure or being rejected that we can override our inspiration to triumph over these fears. Fear will only paralyze the action we should be taking in our lives, causing us to hold ourselves back personally and professionally, settling for far less than we are truly capable of having.

Change, in and of itself, shouldn't be feared, it should be embraced. As spiritual beings having a human experience, we are destined to evolve and expand, which means embracing transformation. Just as it is the nature of the seasons to change, it's the natural order of the universe for us to change.

Changing

Change that arises from the expression of our true, divine-self births something new from within us. This type of change sticks. We behave in new, noticeable ways, we shift the way in which we view some aspect of our lives, such as an old relationship or an old career. We might find ourselves practicing a brand-new value, such as kindness, respect, or integrity. Perhaps we were aware previously of the value of kindness, respect, or integrity, perhaps we talked about the importance of these values. But now, these values are embodied in who we are and how we live our lives. We no longer have to talk about them, we have *become* these values. This new way of being rises from the deepest, most spiritual part of ourselves and changes our lives for the better, forever.

If you don't know what to change in your own life right now, just live your life and when it's time, change will come knocking on your door. We can be assured of this as our soul-self is in complete support of our transformation and evolution. G*o*d and the universe will support us by giving us little nudges that it's time to change; if we can honor those nudges, we'll step naturally into the process of change. If, however, we're not listening—or don't want to listen—then, as we've noted earlier, life will support us fully by bringing us pain.

Being a Catalyst for Change

In this new era of accelerated change, our perception of life is undergoing radical transformation. More than ever before, we are healing, transforming, growing, and expanding. It's one of the ways we contribute to the world—and especially to our own, personal world.

As we expand more and more into our truest selves, many of us will become catalysts to facilitate change in our families, friends, neighbors, employees, and communities. The best way to be a catalyst for others is not by trying to get them to change but rather by staying focused on changing ourselves. Frankly, taking on personal responsibility for changing ourselves ought to be enough! We have the power to change ourselves, we don't have the power to change someone else. And, if we force our power onto someone else to try to get them to change, we'll be met with resistance. The truth is, as we allow others to be who they are and where they're at unconditionally, our own lives become less complicated. And, as we meet others with total acceptance, they feel our unconditional love, and they change. Now, of course, you could assist someone with their transformation and/or healing, if they ask for your help. The most effective way to be a powerful change catalyst for others is to embrace your own change process. When people in your life are ready to change, your willingness to embody the changes that are knocking on your door can inspire them to make changes in their lives as well.

The best way to be a catalyst for others is by changing ourselves.

I love what Sufi mystic Jalaluddin Rumi had to say about change, "Yesterday I was clever, so I wanted to change the world. Today I am wise, so I am changing myself." The world is in genuine need of more of us to become examples of real change. What if we knew that the smallest changes could set the stage for massive transformation in our lives and in the lives of others? Something magical happens in the minds and hearts of those around us as they witness our transformation. Sometimes, the changes we make simply plant seeds for change in another's consciousness that say: *change really can happen once you choose it*. Even though it might not be visible to us right away, when we change ourselves for the better, we change the world for the better. As we transform parts of ourselves and/or our lives, we give others around us permission to embrace change in their lives and to transform.

Becoming Who You Want to Be

Are you happy with the person you are becoming? Are you becoming the best version of yourself? Who do you want to become? These are questions only you can answer. Becoming our best selves is possible for all of us, regardless of our circumstances. For those of us who are willing and ready to accept this responsibility, here's one more practice that we can use at the end of each day. Simply ask yourself: "Was I my best self today? Was I the best husband or the best wife today? The best leader or the best parent? The best manager? The best student? The best man or the best woman? Did I truly strive to be my best self today?"

A quote attributed to the Greek philosopher, Socrates, says, "The secret of all change is to focus all of your energy, not on fighting the old, but on building the new." We break it down day-to-day, we keep it simple, and at the end of each day, we ask, "Did I become my best self today?" We might even, at the start of each day, sit in silence for five minutes—or twenty—and ask ourselves, "Who do I want to become today?"

So, if we're putting on our leadership hat, or our husband or wife hat, or our student hat…whatever that might be, ask, "What would my best self look like today?" "What is the best way for me to be today?" Can we be our best self as we're approaching a new client, our best self at our staff meeting, our best self as we're conversing with one of our children? What does it look like, taking a moment to really connect with our best self at both the start and the end of each day?

You see, when we are our best selves, the possibilities are endless. Remember, by creating this as a focus, always moving towards our best self, we are building anew, instead of always fighting the old. We need desperately to change the old. Remember, our job with the old is to let it go, to let it go in pieces—one layer, one piece at a time—while focusing on where we are going. And then, remember—as we change ourselves, we change our personal worlds. As enough of us choose to change ourselves, together we'll transform our world. This is what we as a society are destined to do. This is our opportunity to turn our world, our planet, into a kinder, better, more peaceful place, and to stop waiting on someone or something to come and do this for us. Might it be possible that we're the ones we've been waiting for? I invite you to watch a video on my YouTube channel titled, *The Many Become One.*

What would it be like to be a part of a beautiful society in which we showed love, compassion, and kindness to one another rather than hate, anger, and judgement? What would it be like if we were to honor our connection to each other, instead of maintaining the disconnect we have created with others? As we come together, we enter into an energy of oneness. This is where our real power is found—in our union with each other, not in our division. This is what makes us stronger as a people, which allows us to explore and embrace the final frontier into the soul.

What if we knew that the world had been waiting for us to awaken? What if we could literally let go of everything we no longer need, and just allow ourselves to be all that we truly are? What would it be like if change were to become second nature to us? What if change were no longer difficult as it simply became the way we lived? *What if?*

And, instead of trying to change one another, or making someone else wrong for wanting to change, what if we were to accept each other as we are? What if we were able to turn our own personal transformation into a lifestyle, inspiring others by our example? What if we as a people were more focused on who we could become, if we were no longer afraid of moving forward in our lives? What if we were accomplishing great things, and every one of us was encouraged in our journey to become our true soul-self? What if we had systems and structures in place designed specifically to lift people up into their greatness? *What if?*

As the members in our society become empowered and come into full expression of their own greatness, we as a society can achieve greatness!

World peace can be achieved as more of us on the planet achieve a sustainable state of inner peace. Today, many of us are choosing what it is we want to be a part of, in what and where we will invest our faith and energy. Will it be Ascension or will it be Apocalypse? *It's up to you.*

As the Buddha once said, "In the end, only three things matter... how much you loved, how gently you lived, and how gracefully you let go of things not meant for you."

I wish you well…and as each day passes, may it become easier for all of us to let go of anything that no longer serves our highest and greatest good, and to continue to grow into our full potential.

Until next time, Godspeed to you and your loved ones. And whenever you can, give a smile to the universe—it will always smile back.

With much love and respect,

Dale

Exercises

For the exercises below, take some quiet time by yourself. Get still. Picture your higher self.

If you don't have an image of your higher self or your soul just yet, picture the words "Higher Self" on the screen of your mind. Place these words right over your heart. With your journal and pen in hand, read these questions. Go with the first answer that comes to you—write it down. Over time, the answers to these questions will change as you change. Be authentic. Stay in the moment—and breathe!

1) Did you experience your true self today? If so, how easy or natural was it for you to experience your true self?

2) Whom in your life has it been easy to express your true self to? What about this person makes it easier for you to express and experience your true self?

3) Are you trying to change anyone today? Who is that person? What is it about this person that you're trying to change? Has any particular need been influencing your desire to change this person (e.g. a need to be right, a need to be safe, or a need for something else)?

4) Is there something you ought to be changing about you / your life, right now? If yes, what is it?

5) If there were three values you could imprint upon humanity that would help humanity move forward, what would they be? Why did you choose these three?

RECOMMENDED READING LIST
(INCLUDES WORKS CITED)

Chessman, Millan. *Cleanse Internally – Controversies, Benefits and Facts*. El Cajon, CA: Smashwords, 2012. Kindle.

Dyer, Wayne W. *Living an Inspired Life – Your Ultimate Calling*. Carlsbad: Hay House, 2006. Print.

--. *Excuses BeGone! How to Change Lifelong, Self-Defeating Thinking Habits*. Carlsbad: Hay House, 2009. Print.

--. *The Power of Intention – Learning to Co-Create Your World Your Way*. Carlsbad: Hay House, 2004. Print.

Emerson, R.W. *The Ultimate Collection*. Copenhagen: Titan Read, nd. Digital.

Epstein, Donald M. *The 12 Stages to Healing – a Network Approach to Wholeness*. Novato: New World Library, 1993. Print.

Jong, Erica. *Fear of Flying*. New York: Penguin, 1973. Print.

Hawkins, David R. *Letting Go – The Pathway of Surrender*. Carlsbad: Hay House, 2012. Print.

Moore, Thomas. *Care of the Soul – A Guide for Cultivating Depth and Sacredness in Everyday Life*. New York: Harper Perennial, 1992. Print.

Montapert, Alfred Armand. *The Supreme Philosophy of Man: The Laws of Life*. nc: Prentice-Hall, 1970. Print.

Pizzorno, Joseph. *The Toxic Solution*. New York: HarperCollins, 2017. Print.

Schuller, Robert H. *The Be (Happy) Attitudes*. New York: Bantam Books, 1987. Print.

--. *Tough Times Never Last, But Tough People Do!* New York: Bantam Books, 1984. Print.

--. *You Can Become the Person You Want to Be!* New York: Jove, 1986. Print.

Shima, Gary J. and Marc S. Herlands. *The Art of Healing – Chronic Illnesses, Obesity and Addictions, with Diet, Nutrition and Alternative Medicine*. nc: Xlibris, 2014. Print.

Singer, Michael A. *The Untethered Soul*. Oakland: New Harbinger Publications, 2007. Print.

Tracy, Brian. *Eat That Frog! 21 Great Ways to Stop Procrastinating and Get More Done in Less Time*. 2nd Edition. San Francisco: Berrett-Koehler, 2007. Print.

--. *The Power of Self-Discipline – 21 Ways to Achieve Lasting Success and Happiness*. Boston: Da Capo Press, 2010. Print.

Tolle, Eckhart. *A New Earth – Awakening to Your Life's Purpose*. New York: Penguin, 2006. Print.

--. *The Power of Now*. Vancouver: Namaste, 1997. Print.

Walker, Norman. *Colon Health – The KEY to a Vibrant Life*. Prescott: Norwalk Press, 1979. Print.

Walsch, Neale Donald. *Conversations with God, Book 1: An Uncommon Dialogue*. New York: G.P. Putnam's Sons, 1995. Print.

--. *Conversations with God, Book 2: An Uncommon Dialogue*. Charlottesville: Hampton Roads, 1997. Print.

--. *Conversations with God, Book 3: An Uncommon Dialogue*. Charlottesville: Hampton Roads, 1998. Print.

--. *Conversations with God, Book 4: Awaken the Species*. Faber: Rainbow Ridge, 2017. Print.

Welwood, John. *Journey of the Heart – Intimate Relationships and the Path of Conscious Love*. New York: Harper Perennial, 1990. Print.

Williamson, Marianne. *The Gift of Change – Spiritual Guidance for Living Your Best Life*. New York: HarperCollins, 2004. Print.

Online Sources:

Halaway, Dale. *The Many Become One*. YouTube: https://www.YouTube.com/watch?v=XfLBCQReXlE

Walsch, Neale Donald. *Living from Your Soul*. 2016. Online seminar: http://EvolvingWisdom.com/ndw/LivingFromYourSoul/digital-course/

Wise Philosophical Quotes:
For quotes from Aristotle, Buddha, Gandhi, Heraclites, Jung, Lao-Tzu, Niebuhr, Roosevelt, Rumi, Shelley, Socrates, Roddenberry (Star Trek), Tolstoy, Twain, and others, please Google *Author Name Quotations*.

ACKNOWLEDGEMENTS

First and foremost, I would like to thank my highest self, my guides, and the Divine for always being there, especially during the writing of this book. A few times sections of the book just disappeared. Once when my teaching schedule was full and I was running behind with the book schedule, I wrote through the night, intending to get caught up. When I went to send the document to the editor that morning, eleven to twelve hours' worth of work vanished the moment I hit the 'send' button. Yet every time these sorts of things happened, once I had fully accepted that *"This is my reality in this moment,"* I was graced with being able to rewrite what was 'lost' in a short period of time. Sometimes rewrites were even better than the sections that had disappeared. Clearly, the power and precision of my higher self and my guides were there all along.

I am deeply grateful to the many people who have supported my work through the years. Some I consider soul family...to name a few: Ernie Karchie, Harvey Crich, Myong Crich, Ray Bechard, Dennis Schmidt, Deborah Schmidt, Peter Johnson, Marilyn Wilson, Jim Cummings, Bob McDonald, Barbara Schriener-Trudel, Enid Singer, David Corbin, Nick KaPande, Anastasia Kurilich, Troy Barnes, Dave Reed, Robert Reed, Aki'Ra Yashiro, Don and Jan Bradley, Genece Hamby, Terry Dibert, Darlene Mae, Janet Franco, Hank and Pat Franco, Gary Havens, Bruce Merrin, Sally St. John, Frank La Spina, David Heil, Tom Shoemaker, Darlene Karn, Ron Greenawalt, Cattel Cattell, Rick Bergen, Ellen Laura, Michelle Hicks-Finnigan, Kristy Jarrett, Mitzi Reed, Robert Reed, Marcel Forestieri, Leslei Fisher, Linda Kidby, Sienna Marie Wise, William Brown, Chris Jarrett, Danielle Barnes, Mindy Buss, Lisa Ulshafer, Nancy O'Connell, Christina Sutton, Kym Figueroa, Sami Sarkis, Matthew Lewis, Janell Lewis, Scott Sutton, Erica Dilanjian, TJ Beatty, Joe Escriba, Loretta Brown, Jennifer Meehan, Bryan Meehan, David Forestieri, Hollie Vest, Julie Quan, Troy Casey, Uri Casey, Jani McCarty, Shantell Thaxton, Alex Thomson, Ragan Thomson-O'Reilly, Candice Park, Alexia Loehde, Charlyn Fernandez, Julee Shea, Forrest Leichtberg, and Mycki Manning.

A shout out and much appreciation to my family: My sisters and their husbands, Debbie and John, Shelly and Dennis; my bro Mark; my daughter Randi and her fiancé Brian; my adopted son TJ; my niece Ashley and her husband Ed and their children, Aiden, Grace, and Zayne; and my nephews, Brett and Jeffrey. I have so many great memories during different phases in our lives together.

Finally, many thanks to the incredible team at Lifestyle Entrepreneurs Press, Jesse Krieger, Kristen Wise, and Michael Ireland...without their creative assistance and loving support this book would not have been possible.

Dale Halaway

CONTINUE YOUR TRANSFORMATION WITH DALE

Thank you for reading my book and for taking the time to invest in your own call to change. I invite you to visit DaleHalaway.com where you'll find valuable products and information that can support you in your awakening and personal transformation and on your journey of self-discovery.

Join our Mailing List

By joining our email list and newsletter, you will receive a new offering every month. This could be a free product such as a meditation or excerpts of my teachings, information about current global events and how to understand them, helpful videos to assist you in navigating real-life situations, and valuable insights to support you in staying awake and aware. My staff and I are always working to bring something of value directly to you—we want to help you to stay on a healing path as you live the life of your dreams.

Radio Show Archives

At the radio show archive link, you'll find talk radio shows where I have been a featured guest, along with excerpts from our own programs. These archives cover a variety of topics, including interviews and questions from listeners. Listening to these Q&A's is a great opportunity to hear my coaching advice and gain valuable insight—you'll find that my guidance for others may also apply to current situations and struggles in your own life.

Live and On-line Seminars

The seminars I have developed over my forty years of teaching are available online and in-person presentations. At the core of each seminar are the Universal Laws, and each program teaches you to apply a unique process that will help you release subconscious programming, unblock restricted energy flow, and move forward in your life. The seminars cover many different topics. In the *Relationship N' You*™ seminar series, we examine our relationships—not just with people, but with money, business, home, and pets. Our success in both private life and in business is examined in the *Gateway to Success*™ courses; solutions for financial issues and subconscious programming surrounding money are revealed in the *Mastery with Money*™ seminars; resolving and releasing the karma we have created (and could continue to create depending upon our actions in this lifetime) is examined in the *Karmic Destiny*™ courses; and the *TransCovery Experience*™ teaches qualified students how to become a coach for family and friends and is a precursor to my in-depth training series for becoming a professional certified coach. Whether you want to develop your personal, professional, or spiritual life further, there is a seminar and a body of teachings that will complement the area you want to improve.

Webinars

At the webinars link, you'll find ongoing, complimentary webinars that correlate with the seminar offerings listed above. These webinars cover a variety of topics and each one has a Q&A at the end. The Q&A's contain questions concerning real-life situations attendees are going through— and everyone can benefit from the coaching I offer. How we handle and interact with each of these webinar topics determines much of what happens in our outer world. The subconscious programs we carry in relation to our life's challenges are revealed in each of the courses and I provide a simple toolkit to help you recognize, work through, and clear these blockages. Do you want to lead a more fulfilling life and career? I invite you to join our webinars and to learn more about what you can do to make the most out of every aspect of your life.

The TransCovery Process®

The TransCovery Process® was designed to help you release the subconscious programming that is blocking your energy flow. I developed this method over a number of years in my work with many different types of people from many different walks of life. This technique is integrated into all of my teachings and once learned, it takes on average less than three minutes to do. It is a remarkable way to manage your thoughts and feelings through a series of specific questions in a specific sequence. When used on a regular basis, it can help you progress and move forward to greater inner peace and abundance, and become the greatest version of you—the you that you are meant to be. Please refer to our website for a more detailed description of *The TransCovery Process*® and what it can do for You.

Keynote Speaking for your Event

For almost forty years I have been a speaker and trainer for the private and corporate sectors. My direct work with a wide range of individuals from CEOs and entrepreneurs to entertainers gives me a large experiential base to draw from in customizing an engaging presentation and/or training program that will empower and elevate your group. I have extensive knowledge and experience in analytics, interactive strategic planning, entrepreneurial training, transformational leadership, inspirational keynotes, conflict resolution/mediation, and team unification. If you are looking for a speaker or teacher to bring value to your event, I could be the right fit for you.

Private Intensives and Business Coaching

I have spent many years serving as a coach for corporations and for private individuals. Though I am not taking on new coaching clients on a private basis, I offer private intensives and business coaching programs in which I use my many years of coaching, teaching, and facilitation experience to help corporations, celebrities, influential leaders, and private clientele meet the challenges of business and life. If having a private, customized intensive or business coaching program resonates with you, I invite you to inquire through the Services section of our website.

TransMeditation Series™

Taken from my seminars, this meditation series is derived from my highly effective Sunday morning meditations. The meditations consist of three parts, each having a specific purpose that tie together to create a powerful and effective experience. The first part helps you clear out resistance by raising your awareness of limiting dynamics; the second part incorporates *The Transcovery Process*® to help you release all that no longer serves you; and the third part is a visualization that helps you connect to your higher self, the ascended masters, and the angelic realm. These meditations help you both to stay centered and to re-center quickly. Each has a specific theme and purpose and can be used as and when needed. The meditations in this series are frequency-modulated, taking you deeply into a meaningful personal experience—you will discover something of profound value about yourself when you use these meditations!

As you can see, after you set this book down, there is a great deal to support you further as you progress in your life and answer the Call to Change. I look forward to helping provide some of that support and to having a continuing relationship with you. Thank you for taking the time to learn more about me and for taking the time to read my book.

More books are available in the Transformation Trilogy series. Please refer to my website for other books and offerings from my life's work in awakening and evolving those who are Being Called to Change.

Many blessings,

Dale Halaway

TRANSFORMATION
Trilogy

Begin Your Transformation:
www.DaleHalaway.com

CPSIA information can be obtained
at www.ICGtesting.com
Printed in the USA
LVHW01s0303070318
568775LV00003B/3/P